CT

/Doterel class sloop,
heerness Dockyard, 1878.

oration at the Historic
Chatham.

Length B.P.	170 ft.
Breadth, Moulded	36 ft.
Draught, Max.	15 ft. 9in.
Rig	Barque
Machinery	Humphreys and Tennant, 2 cylinder 2 stage horizontal steam reciprocating engine.
Armament	2 × 7 in RML
	3 × 64 pdr. RML
	2 × 5in BL
Complement	140

Medway College of Art

HMS
GANNET

HMS
GANNET
Ship and Model

William Mowll

FOREWORD BY FRED WALKER

Seaforth
PUBLISHING

For Susie, my true love these fifty years and more.

Copyright © William Mowll 2018

First published in Great Britain in 2018 by
Seaforth Publishing,
A division of Pen & Sword Books Ltd,
47 Church Street,
Barnsley S70 2AS

www.seaforthpublishing.com

British Library Cataloguing in Publication Data
A catalogue record for this book is available from the British Library
ISBN 978 1 5267 2628 5 (HARDBACK)
ISBN 978 1 5267 2629 2 (EPUB)
ISBN 978 1 5267 2630 8 (KINDLE)

All illustrations and photographs are from the author's collection
unless otherwise stated.

The right of William Mowll to be identified as the author of this
work has been asserted by him in accordance with the Copyright,
Designs and Patents Act 1988.

Pen & Sword Books Limited incorporates the imprints of Atlas,
Archaeology, Aviation, Discovery, Family History, Fiction,
History, Maritime, Military, Military Classics, Politics, Select,
Transport, True Crime, Air World, Frontline Publishing, Leo
Cooper, Remember When, Seaforth Publishing,
The Praetorian Press, Wharncliffe Local History, Wharncliffe
Transport, Wharncliffe True Crime and White Owl

Typeset and designed by Neil Sayer
Printed by Printworks Global Ltd., London & Hong Kong

Contents

Foreword

Throughout my life it has been a delight and privilege to view some of the best ship-model collections in the world, and over many years I have developed an ever-growing appreciation of this skilled art and craft. During my time at the National Maritime Museum, Greenwich, it became clear that while model collections have many purposes, the most important function is as an aid to teaching and education. On first seeing William Mowll's model of HMS *Gannet*, I was amazed not only at the world-class standard of workmanship, but also that he had captured – most successfully – the elusive spirit of this ship.

I have been associated with *Gannet* for many years, and from 2000–2006 was the directing naval architect of the team assembled at Chatham Historic Dockyard for the refurbishment of this naval sloop, now nearing 140 years in age. The restoration team worked throughout in great harmony and the ship was completed on time and within budget. Using twenty-first-century model-making technology, William Mowll has built a model of the composite constructed steam-powered gun vessel of the nineteenth century. Planned in every detail,

the model *Gannet* gives us a glimpse into the lives and work of the seafaring men and of the Royal Navy which protected British trade and worldwide interests before the Great War.

Fred M Walker

Formerly Consulting Naval Architect, the National Maritime Museum, Greenwich

Acknowledgements

Acknowledgements and gratitude are owed to the following, in alphabetical order: Richard Briggs (TS *Mercury* Old Boys' Association); Richard Chasemore, engine and boiler illustration; Andrew Choong, Plans Service, National Maritime Museum, Greenwich, London; John Cundell, former editor of *Model Boats*; Malcolm Darch FSNR; Bill Ferris OBE, Chief Executive, CHDT; Jeff Frier CENG FRINA; Peter Hillman (TS *Mercury* OBA); Richard Holdsworth MBE, Museum Director, Chatham Historic Dockyard; Michael Kosten, Editor, *Ships in Scale*; Michael E Leek, author and illustrator; Mike Lee, *Inflexible* and coppering; Julian Mannering, Editorial Director, Seaforth Publishing; Roger Marsh, European Editor, *Ships in Scale*; Ken Martin, Chief Operating Officer, The American Philatelic Society; Ben Mowll RMSA, marine artist; Josh Mowll, author, photographer and CGI graphics; T Nielsen and Co Ltd, Shipbuilders, Glos Docks; Stanley Paine ARCA; John Regan, sculptor in miniature figures; Dr Alistair Roach, author; Dr Stephanie Rudgard-Redsell, for bringing order out of chaos in editing the material for this book; Stephen Saunders, son of the last bursar of TS *Mercury*; Steve Taylor, technical consultant in GRP lamination; Fred M Walker, author and naval architect i/c *Gannet* restoration programme in association with BMT Ship Design, also consulting naval architect to the NMM Greenwich; Adrian L White, *TS Mercury History, 1885–1968* (2003); M White, former student at the Medway College of Art *c*1990, for the coloured ship's illustration; Cdr Alastair Wilson RN, naval historian (HMS *Warrior*).

Internal details on all three deck levels of HMS *Gannet* (1878) model at a scale of 1:48 – a glimpse of how a full-scale restoration would appear.

Introduction

Why *Gannet* and why a model of this ship? To answer the two questions, there is a need to appreciate a relatively recent change in mood and attitude towards the preservation of nautical and naval history in UK. The fresh thinking really began with a single letter, written by Dr E C B Corlett to *The Times* newspaper in 1967, with a plea to our maritime nation to rescue SS *Great Britain* (1843) from the Falkland Islands before it was too late. This famous ship, designed by Isambard Kingdom Brunel, was in a shocking state of decay, with only months left before disintegration beyond repair.

That seminal letter was met initially with a ready response by certain individuals and started a new wave of interest in preserving the nation's four very special transitional ships, starting with *Great Britain*, quickly followed by HMS *Warrior* (1860), the total refurbishment of the Antarctic exploring ship SS *Discovery* (1901), and finishing with the repair and restoration in this century of HMS *Gannet* (1878). These ships were all formerly powered by steam and sail, and each of them in their different locations was just surviving, more by chance than usage.

Tourism is the other reason for their survival. Without the renewed emphasis we now place on visitor destinations, they would not have any reason to be maintained as exhibition pieces which have significantly altered the way major cities such as Bristol, Portsmouth, Dundee and Chatham have developed as tourist attractions, and each one of these ships is now presented as a prime exhibit for visitors from all over the world. They stand as talismans of pure wonder for the triumphs achieved by British nineteenth-century ship designers, builders and engineers.

From the 1970s to the 1990s, financial support for these rescue and restoration initiatives was very difficult to find, and despite what the general public may regard as high entry-ticket prices to see these wonders of a bygone age, not a single one of them would ever be able survive without extra funding. The Heritage Lottery Fund has now touched each of these preserved ships, and whilst money is still tight, they do now enjoy life and status as the proud possessions of the cities where they lie in state, rather than being strange obscurities from a past age which are of no general interest to anyone. Intriguingly, they also appeal to a wider spectrum of interests where the restoration has included the social life of the ship, with their interior furnishings and domestic details thus encompassing social and cultural history, in addition to naval history. A highly polished wardroom table and chairs with correctly laid place settings ornamented with silver cutlery, napkin rings and cut-glass decanters, all evoking a bygone age, have an appeal for many visitors which goes well beyond the serried ranks of heavy ordnance neatly arranged along a gun deck.

It is this last point which brings me directly to answering the second question of why a model of *Gannet* when the real ship is on display at Chatham Dockyard? At the very outset of making a detailed and scaled model of this ship, my intention is to fill the information gap aboard *Gannet*, where all the visitor will see, to date, is the void of an empty shell. What the full-sized *Gannet* lacks in her interior fittings, with the absence of the steam engine, three boilers and other internal details, it is hoped that the model will help illustrate and inform.

There are two stages to rescuing a ship – one is to prevent her from falling to pieces, which by simple neglect and decay can so easily happen and the other is to show to the visitor an exhibit from which people can learn and understand how life aboard was lived and how the ship was managed and operated. That is what a full restoration achieves.

THE UK'S COLLECTION OF SAIL AND STEAM-ASSISTED SHIPS — THE TRANSITIONALS IN HISTORICAL ORDER OF THEIR RESTORATION

We are extraordinarily fortunate in the United Kingdom to have as permanent exhibits, open to the public throughout the year, *Great Britain*, *Warrior*, *Discovery* and *Gannet*, four outstanding ships all very different from one another, but each of which shares a short period of nautical history when steam and sail went cheek by jowl, with all the joys and difficulties this presented to those who had to operate and sail them. As a group of vessels, they ushered in an entirely new concept of reliable scheduled water transport, no longer dependent on the vagaries of the weather. Their new status, however, had the serious disadvantage that they were burdened in the best quarters of the ship with noisy machinery, soot in the sails and the need to bunker large quantities of steaming coal, occupying space which in a conventional sailing ship would earn their owners good money. Commercially speaking, speed had overtaken capacity.

PS *SIRIUS* (1837) AND PS *GREAT WESTERN* (1837)

The paddle ship *Sirius* predates the surviving quartet, and her story sadly ended by being lost in the fog on 16 June 1847 and wrecked on the rocky shores of Ballycotton Bay in southern Ireland. She never completed her final journey from Glasgow to Cork. It was the end of her, but it is where my story as an adult ship-modeller begins in 1977.

I had seen a model of this attractive steam and sailing ship, first in a book and then in the Science Museum, London; it was chosen by me as a subject simply because here was a vessel into whose hull a miniature steam plant would be easy to place, fit and operate, and I loved the look of that tall, thin funnel. The model was built for my two boys, then aged seven and ten, and the story was picked up by the UK magazine *Model Boats*, whose editor was keen to learn more about the building of the miniature working replica and her history. This was my first venture into the world of publication; up to this point in my life, I thought

PS *Sirius* (1837): author's steam-powered model of the first ship to cross the Atlantic from Britain to America under continuous steam power, arriving on 23 April 1838. This model is now housed in the American Philatelic Society building, Pennsylvania, USA.

that publishing one's work was something other people did, nor had I made the connection in my mind between ships and their historical significance, a subject which now fascinates me. The paddle-ship *Sirius*, as I discovered, snatched the Atlantic crown away from Isambard Kingdom Brunel's much larger and better-equipped paddle steamer PS *Great Western* (1837), the first steamship built and designed for the Atlantic run, and also the only one of Brunel's ships that turned in a regular profit for the Great Western Steamship Company. The rakish little *Sirius* managed, by the skin of her teeth, to cross the Atlantic from Cork in southern Ireland to New York under continuous steam power, arriving exhausted in Sandy Hook Bay early on Monday, 23 April 1838, and anchored in the North River immediately off the Battery. The voyage had taken eighteen days, four hours and twenty-two minutes, with ninety-four cabin passengers.

Great Western arrived on the same day in the afternoon, having set out three days later than *Sirius*. A crowd of New Yorkers were lined up on the quayside, anticipating the arrival of Brunel's ship, but instead found themselves cheering home a completely different vessel. The New York press described the scene: 'Nothing could exceed the excitement. The river was covered during the whole day with row-boats, skiffs and yawls carrying the wondering people out to get a close view of this extraordinary vessel. While people were yet wondering how the *Sirius* so successfully made out, to cross the rude Atlantic, it was announced about 11.00am on Monday, from the telegraph that a huge steamship was in the offing – "The *Great Western*! The *Great Western*!" was on everybody's tongue.'

RESCUE OF THE PRESERVED SHIPS IN THE UK

Between 1978 and 1981 the model of *Great Britain* was built and, as with all my model ships (except for *Warrior*), I used what is called the 'plank on frame' method, whereby miniature planks are applied to bulkhead frames, following the body line plan and giving the resultant hull its distinctive shape. It is not quite what happens in full-scale shipbuilding, but the method produces an acceptably accurate representation of the prototype for a working model.

The second preserved traditional ship, *Warrior*, was in 1982 just beginning a total reconstruction at the Coal Dock Wharf in West Hartlepool. Her all-iron hull was sound, but other areas were little short of ghastly after fifty long years of acting as a pontoon for oil tankers, mooring up alongside her at Llanion fuel depot (Pembroke dock) both to refuel and discharge their cargo. She was at that time totally unrecognisable from what visitors see today. You have to admire the astonishing challenge that the team of restorers in West Hartlepool faced in those early days. They almost literally brought her back from the dead, urged on by the financial backing provided by her saviour Sir John Smith,

Above: PS *Great Western:* arrival in New York.

Below: The first rescue, 1970: SS *Great Britain* (1843) was the first ship of the preserved transitional ships now resident in the UK. Author's working model of Brunel's *Great Britain* in the 1846 rig, placed in the Brunel Institute Library, alongside the prototype in the dockyard at Bristol, UK.

formerly an MP for the cities of London and Westminster (1965–70) and chairman of the Manifold Trust, who largely funded her rebuilding into the ship we see today.

Gannet was launched from the Royal Naval Dockyard at Sheerness in Kent, UK, coming down the slip on 31 August 1878. As with so many of these composite vessels designed by Nathaniel Barnaby, at that time chief architect of the Royal Navy, she was by no means unique. In total there were fourteen ships in her class built between 1876 and 1880 and although they all enjoyed the same basic specifications, some of the *Osprey/Doterel* class had a bow with a straight stem; others, like *Gannet* and *Osprey*, were built with the much more graceful clipper bow.

Gannet as a gun vessel is not merely a survivor of her class, but also represents the only remaining example of well over a hundred warships built at Sheerness during the long and distinguished service of that royal dockyard. There is, sadly, almost nothing left of the original dockyard site these days, where once it was a major centre of activity. By the turn of the twentieth century, the Admiralty had reorganised the dockyard mainly for the fitting and maintenance of warships, with a great emphasis on torpedo boats, which

were quite rightly seen as the new weapon of choice against the rising threat of warships being built in Germany. Sheerness launched their last built ship in 1902.

In her state as launched, *Gannet* appeared rather different from the way she looks now, having no raised quarterdeck fitted, and only a flying bridge for conning the ship; the poop and other refinements were added in the major refit of 1885, and her present appearance follows these later plans, from whose details the model was also built.

RESEARCH

My research on the *Gannet* began in 2013, and some of the most interesting and illuminating research for the model arose from personal contact with those involved in restoring the full-size ship.

I was able to consult Richard Holdsworth, Preservation and Education Director at Chatham and Chris Jones, the man called upon for the daily practical issues which the dockyard presents, and with his own particular interest in *Gannet*.

You will read in the acknowledgements the name of Commander Alastair Wilson RN, who has been at the heart of many projects to do with ship restoration in the UK. I first met him in connection with HMS *Warrior*, of which he is the current historian, but he had also been involved in the

HMS *Warrior* (1860), returned to Portsmouth. Original watercolour painting by Benjamin Mowll, 15 June 2007.

The second rescue, 1979: the author's working steam-powered model of *Warrior* (1:48 scale) sailing in the English Channel. The model, which is over 3m (10ft) in length, is now on permanent display at Portsmouth Historic Dockyard.

early days of Chatham Dockyard's new role as an officially recognised National Heritage Site after the Royal Navy's departure. It was he who introduced me to Fred M Walker, the man chosen to be the official naval architect for the whole of *Gannet*'s restoration programme. After what I can only describe as one of the most intriguing and engaging meetings of my life, Mr Walker loaned me the equivalent of 'gold, frankincense and myrrh': namely the 1885 ship's plans, the original Admiralty Specifications for the building of the ship, and the Draft Conservation Plan, prepared for and accepted by the Heritage Lottery Fund. These are the three documents which lie at the very heart of this book.

Late in the building project of the *Gannet* model I was also able to meet Tommi Nielsen of T Nielsen & Company, the specialist shipbuilders undertaking the restoration project. With an astonishing generosity of spirit this busy shipbuilder, surrounded by the paraphernalia of a working dockyard, in a highly personalised office steeped in the work and detail of many traditionally restored yachts and barges

still on the water today in the UK, was prepared to give his precious time to an amateur model-maker whom he had never previously met. The gentle nature and enthusiasm of Tommi Nielsen shone through his every word. Humility is the key to greatness, and when asked what was the most difficult aspect of the reconstruction, he simply replied, 'Interpreting the plans.' I was also introduced to Dominic Mills and Nigel Patrick, who had worked on the project. They gave me the sort of details which can only be provided by true witnesses, present and hands on, during the whole venture in the dockyard at Chatham. I learned from them of the foul stench of machining masts and yards which had been seasoned in the mast pond for three years; of the pitch and tar paper used as insulation under the 12 tons of 'peppered' copper sheathing, which they were required to remove; of the difficulty of working the tropical hardwood called opepe used on the poop deck and stern; of the heavy metal work and wrought iron fittings, all cast on site in the Gloucester works. It was a privilege to be speaking twelve years later to those who had been present at the time – their record of exactly what took place could so easily have been lost in the intervening years. One of my final questions to them was what was their reaction on hearing that Nielsen's had won the contract to restore *Gannet*? With the broad grin of a successful conqueror and looking towards his colleague, Dominic replied, 'It was the biggest project we

Above: Third yard rescue, 1985: SS *Discovery* (1901). The author's partly built static model photographed in 2010, depicting the kind of conditions with which the Antarctic explorers were faced in the ice-fields of the South Pole. This model was built as a commission in my retirement and is privately owned.

Below: In the model wardroom of *Discovery*. Lieutenant Charles Royds entertained the ship's company every night between 1700 and 1800 hours. He was a fine musician and raised the spirits of the whole crew with his playing. The miniature figure was sculpted by John Regan. The original organ is preserved at Discovery Point Museum, Dundee.

The completed model of SS *Discovery* (1901). She was designated a Royal Research Ship (RRS) in 1923, when she was refitted in preparation for the 1925 Antarctic Oceanographic expedition.

Fourth rescue, 2000: HMS *Gannet* undergoing restoration in No. 4 Dock, Chatham, on 26 August 2003.

had ever been asked to tackle and we were up for it.' I was then offered the equivalent of the Crown jewels, with the simple question – 'Would you like a memory stick of the photos we took during the project?' I left Gloucester Docks that morning in a state of high elation, knowing that their record would greatly enhance the material I was trying to gather together.

Being able to talk to all of these most knowledgeable and helpful participants in the restoration of *Gannet*, all of whom had such direct and relevant experience which they were so kindly willing to share, has contributed greatly to my work on the model, and the end result has been much enhanced by their generosity.

The Launch of
HMS *Gannet* took
place on 31
August 1878 at
HM Dockyard
Sheerness. This
picture was taken
much later, c1890.
(© National
Maritime
Museum,
Greenwich,
London, P47591)

Gannet the
model in the
display case,
2 August 2017.

Gannet in all her glory, resplendent and newly restored at Chatham Dockyard, 2004.

1: The History of *Gannet*

HMS *GANNET* AND HMS *INFLEXIBLE* – BEAUTY AND THE BEAST

Two individual, but very different, warships, *Inflexible* (1876) and *Gannet* (1878) were designed by the same man, Nathaniel Barnaby, who was at this time appointed under the new title of Director of Naval Construction to the Royal Navy. The differing designs exactly describe what was going on in the mid to late nineteenth-century Royal Navy as far as the thinking and planning for the next phase of British naval development are concerned. In 1876 'Britannia ruled the waves' and *Inflexible* with her mighty muzzle-loading guns stands for naval experiments of every kind, and greatly pleased those who believed that the all-big-gun ship was the future for the British Empire, both on the offensive front for the ever-expanding dominions, and also in defence of the nation. Within three days of the launch of *Inflexible* in 1876, Queen Victoria took the title Empress of India.

Little *Gannet* and her associates, on the other hand, existed to enforce the peace of Pax Britannica and she was representative of all those who wanted the dream of Empire kept alive. She was part of the necessary and required floating police force for the newly gained territories, which now included India; by comparison with the latest armoured battleships of the Black Battlefleet, the composite-built *Gannet* was cheap to run, and could run for a very long way on very little. The Mediterranean all-white livery and gracious lines of *Gannet*'s hull is in ultimate contrast with *Inflexible*'s menacing exterior; *Gannet*'s displacement weight is almost exactly one-tenth of that of *Inflexible*.

The *Inflexible*-class turret battleship represents the thinking not only of the Admiralty, but also of the British nation – a floating fortress with the most powerful muzzle-loading guns ever fitted to any vessel, protected by the thickest armoured belt carried by any ship, even to this present day. This brute of a battleship's hull was constructed from wrought iron, sporting the latest style of low freeboard popular with the new breed of battleships, representing in all aspects the floating muscle-power of the British Empire. She is the successor to the Black Battlefleet of the Channel, and initially, like her elder sisters, was fully masted and rigged. In theory, at least, she would be the first of a new concept in ship design which would be a match for the Italian *Duilio* (1876) and would give renewed protection for the British nation.

By contrast, the nomination of vessels which *Gannet* represents, of wading birds, psychologically gives the game away. These 'colonial cruisers', although they are fully armed naval vessels, appear silently sailing along the shoreline or in an estuary into shallow water in an unobtrusive way, offering first an olive branch rather than a well-aimed broadside. They speak not of war, but of possible peace, a gentle policing tactic on foreign shores, where a whisky and soda shared with the captain in the well-appointed wardroom would be a far more effective policy of deterrent with the local chieftains and warlords than any shore-based skirmish using offensive weapons. Sloops of war could fight, but that was not the point of these gun vessels, because the British Empire by this time was becoming so vast that no one wanted to start a fresh war with unintended consequences.

So here we have the two faces of the Royal Navy – the first representing the ever-changing patterns and novelty in the new breed of warship with all their offensive weaponry and experimental gear, and secondly, the quiet peacekeeping role of these virginal white sailing vessels which speak softly of the good sense of sweet reason, as opposed to noisy pitched naval battles and seemingly endless blockades.

SIR NATHANIEL BARNABY

Nathaniel Barnaby served the Admiralty for almost his entire career. After working at Woolwich Dockyard as a draughtsman, he joined the staff of Sir Edward Reed, and at

1

Sir Nathaniel Barnaby, designer of both *Gannet* and *Inflexible*. (RINA)

GANNET DATA

Overall length: 190ft
Perpendicular length: 170ft
Beam: 36ft
Draught: 16ft; draught mean: 14ft 6in
Mainmast height from keel to truck: 132ft
Approximate weight of hull: 630 tons
Displacement: 1,130 tons
Machinery: 2-cylinder horizontal compound expansion
   steam engine (Humphrys Tennant & Co, Deptford)
Weight of engine: 45 tons
Boilers: 3 x 15ft cylindrical fire tube boilers; working
   pressure 60psi
Speed: 15 knots under sail; 12.5 knots under steam
Range under steam: 2,014 nautical miles @ 11.5 knots
   (7.3 days); 3,240 nautical miles @ 5 knots (27 days)
Indicated HP: 1,128
Propeller: Griffiths patent twin-bladed hoisting screw, 13ft
   1in
Revolutions per minute: 100
Speed on first trial, 20 Jan 1879: 2.953 knots per hour
Coal bunker capacity: 140 tons

Barque rigged: original sail area 9,940 sq ft
Complement: 13 officers & warrant officers; 27 petty
   officers; 64 seamen; 11 boys; 24 marines
Armament: two 7in rifled muzzle-loaders (90cwt guns);
   four 64pdr rifled muzzle-loaders mounted broadside
   (reduced to three in 1885, with one as the bow chaser
   under the fo'c'sle and the other two mounted on racer
   arcs just aft the funnel). 5in CP mounted
   Vavasseur/Armstrong guns were used as stern-chasers,
   attached to the poop sponsons in the 1885 refit.
   Nordenfelt machine guns were added in 1885;
   provision for eight mounted positions provided
   throughout the ship. Two five-barrelled Gardner
   machine guns 0.45 calibre. Hand weapons included
   Henri Martini rifles
Ship's boats: one 25ft steam cutter; one 30ft cutter; two
   27ft whalers; one 16ft jolly boat; one 12ft dinghy
Cost of building and completing for sea: hull £39,581;
   cost of propelling and other machinery £12,889; other
   works and fittings £4,820; total cost £57,290

an early age was singled out for promotion. In 1872, whilst still in his early forties, he was appointed Chief Constructor of the Navy, a position he held until 1885, by which time it had been redesignated Director of Naval Construction (DNC), making him the first man to hold this distinguished post. During his thirteen years at the helm, the Royal Navy took delivery of some interesting ships, whilst experimenting with steel, armour plating and different forms of bracketless construction, a forerunner of longitudinal framing. There was a mild flirtation with composite construction, and several sloops (some later redesignated as corvettes) were built, *Gannet* being the only one of which has been restored.

FIRST COMMISSION: PACIFIC STATION, 17 APRIL 1879 – 20 JULY 1883

Gannet was commissioned on 17 April 1879 and set sail from Portsmouth under the command of Edmund G Burke, her captain, and the flag of Admiral de Horsey, crossing the Atlantic and bound for the port of Panama, arriving in the Pacific in 1880. This long trip, made via the Straits of Magellan route, gave the ship a thorough proving and shaking down. She had been called to the Pacific Station in a response to a declared war between the nations of Peru and Chile, which had taken place the year before in 1879.

The serious sea battles of Iquique and Angamos are now officially known as the War of the Pacific. Fierce fighting had broken out in May 1879 between the nations of Bolivia and

Peru on one side, and Chile on the other. The flashpoint was over increased taxation for the export of nitrate fertiliser from Bolivia and Peru, but there had already been a simmering resentment building up between these rival nations during the previous six years, which had now reached boiling point. The Royal Navy became involved because the Bolivian president, having only a blockaded navy of his own, had offered letters of marque to any ships prepared to join in the conflict on the Bolivian/Peruvian side. The United States, Britain and France allied themselves to Chile against Peru and Bolivia. The allies did so because all three nations had recently signed up to a treaty in Paris declaring a respect for maritime law, which had outlawed the use of letters of marque.

The blockaded Bolivian/Peruvian fleet possessed a prize British-built ship, the turret-firing *Huascar* (1865), purchased before their finances were at rock bottom. They also had an iron frigate named *Independencia* (1874). The rival Chileans matched these vessels with some serious, central battery, iron-clad frigates, a corvette, a gunboat and some monitors purchased from the United States after the close of the American War of Independence. The two sides were relatively well-matched, except that the Chilean ships had a greater range of fire and better armour protection.

The naval engagement of Iquique was fought in May 1879, followed quickly by the battle of Angamos in October 1879, in which the Peruvian fleet was decimated. This all took place before the arrival of *Gannet*. Although fighting

2

'General Quarters', HMS *Kingfisher* (1879). *Kingfisher* was a composite-built ship very similar to *Gannet*, also launched from Sheerness in 1879, powered by Maudslay engines. She was armed, as per *Gannet*, with the later pattern of 90cwt MLR broadside guns as seen in the picture. (© National Maritime Museum, Greenwich, London, A3604)

continued in this part of the world, the Pacific war was technically over by 1884, and ships like *Gannet* played only a shadowing role in the aftermath, with no shots fired in anger. She did witness the scuttling of the Peruvian fleet – an attempt to stop the fleet falling into enemy hands, and at her station, standing off Valparaiso, protected British interests and trade; she was also responsible for feeding reports of events to the *Illustrated London News*. By July 1883 *Gannet* had returned to pay off at her home port of Sheerness,

having sailed over 60,000 miles on her first commission. As a postscript to this account, Admiral de Horsey, as the most senior military figure in the conflict, found himself both the subject of a formal diplomatic protest from the Peruvian government for his naval attack on their iron-clad frigate *Huascar*, and also, in the aftermath of the second battle, he was required to give an explanation to the British Parliament of why he had failed to capture her! It did no harm to his future career.

3

Gannet: the ship's band. Note the young doe mascot in front of the bass drum. (Chatham Historic Dockyard Trust)

Huascar saw further action against the British later in 1887, and has proved to be another sole surviving example of her age. She is today maintained as a shrine to the Peruvian and Chilean navies at Talcahuano navy base in Chile. As an all-iron British-built frigate, although much smaller, she shares some similarity in structure and build with HMS *Warrior* (1860), and was likewise powered by John Penn engines.

REFIT 1883–1885, SHEERNESS

After her adventures in the Pacific, between 1883 and 1885 *Gannet* was stripped down for a serious two-year refit, during which time the original flying bridge was removed and the main deck enclosed at the extremes. These alterations included adding new iron deck beams to the fo'c'sle, in which the 64cwt bow-chaser gun was housed; this had the advantage of giving the ship the possibility of forward fire from the embrasures port and starboard, and better protection for the gun crew. At the aft end of the ship, a new wardroom was created by building over the original quarterdeck, providing the ship with a poop deck. Other refinements included a bed space for the commander on the port side of the wardroom, space for a dining table

which doubled as a chart table, a warming stove and some deeply buttoned chaises longues furnishings occupying the internal sweep of the quarter galleries. At this time greater concern was also given to the 'heads' of the ship for seamen, warrant officers and senior officers, all of whom now had separate designated areas for their private needs, a comment on the social order of the day. The poop deck received the latest navigational aids and at the centre of the curvaceous decking midships now stood the helm compass, engine telegraphs and voice pipes. The two-handed helm wheel remained below the poop deck, but now afforded some shelter for the helmsmen. Wing sponsons were created for the central pivot 5in Armstrong breech-loading guns, mounted on the outer edges of the poop deck as covering fire for the ship's stern.

The propelling machinery remained unaltered, nor were the boilers replaced, which gives rise to the thought that on her first commission they were not over-used but well maintained.

SECOND COMMISSION: WAR IN THE SUDAN, 3 SEPTEMBER 1885 – 1 NOVEMBER 1888

Gannet was recommissioned from her home port of Sheerness in September 1885 and, commanded by Commander Barton Rose Bradford, she set sail for the Mediterranean Station at Malta. For the following three years she was used in the role of fleet support, mainly on anti-slavery patrols in the Red Sea where the practice of

4

Mr Williams on the quarterdeck of *Gannet*. (Chatham
Historic Dockyard Trust)

slavery was still rife. She was once again back in Malta
harbour for a mid-commission refit in September 1888,
when issued with urgent orders to join the squadron
protecting the Sudanese port of Suakin on the shoreline of
the Red Sea, relieving her counterpart HMS *Dolphin* (1882)
of her duties.

Suakin was a strategic and fortified port under Egyptian
control and administration, with British and Indian troops
landed there in 1885 to defend the territory. Three years
later the whole district had been completely over-run by the
rebel forces of a local dervish warlord named Osman Digna.
These rebels were allied to the Islamic Mahdist forces
responsible for the fall of Khartoum and the death of
General Gordon three years earlier in January 1885.

The fort at Suakin was an important military post for both
the British Army and the Royal Navy and its loss to the local
Dervish forces caused an uproar in the British Parliament. The
opening of the Suez canal six years previously in 1869 added
to the significance of Suakin's key position at the foot of the
Red Sea; this had drastically intensified after the fall of
Khartoum in 1885. There was already a plan in place in 1884
to build an overland railway to the military station at Berger,
280 miles due west of Suakin, rather than troops having to use
the hazardous River Nile as an evacuation route. A section of

twenty miles of track through the Red Sea Hills from Suakin
cost an initial £1 million, leaving a further unbuilt section of
260 miles before reaching Berber. The proposed cost of
completion caused a further political row, partly responsible
for the end of Gladstone's second term in office. With the
contractors departed and the work left unguarded, the Arabs
and the local rains destroyed the rest.

Suakin's occupation by the local Sudanese warlords was
Gannet's opportunity to restore order, and she took it on 17
September 1888 by first opening fire with her poop-
mounted 5in guns in support of land forces against an attack
by Osman Digna's rebels. During the following twenty-seven
days *Gannet*'s main armament fired over two hundred shells,
and her Nordenfelt machine guns fired nearly 1,200 rounds
in the defence of Suakin, thus securing the fort once again.
The siege was lifted but it took a further two months to
finally defeat the Mahdist sympathisers. *Gannet*'s visit to
Suakin was short-lived – less than a month – and, in need of
fresh provisions and ammunition, she was relieved on 15
October by the composite gunboat HMS *Starling* (1882) and
paid off the following month at Malta on 1 November 1888.

THIRD COMMISSION: SURVEYING THE MEDITERRANEAN, 10 NOVEMBER 1888 – DECEMBER 1891

With almost undue haste, *Gannet* was recommissioned for
the third time on 10 November 1888 after only nine days in
port, commanded by Commander H Corfe. She spent the

5

Watercolour of *Gannet* in Dockyard Creek, Grand Harbour Malta, from Ian Marshall's book, *Cruisers and La Guerre de Course*, Mystic Seaport, 2007. (Reproduced with the kind permission of Jean Marshall)

6

Gannet in 1891, Malta outer harbour. (© National Maritime Museum, Greenwich, London, D 4311)

next three years surveying the Mediterranean, adding details to British Admiralty charts which, since the time of the navigator and explorer Captain James Cook a hundred years earlier, were regarded with the deepest veneration and trust on account of their being constantly updated for accuracy and dependability.

FOURTH COMMISSION: HYDROGRAPHICS, 26 JANUARY 1892 – 16 MARCH 1895

Still stationed at Malta, *Gannet's* final commission on active service, commanded by F F Fergen, engaged with the relatively new discipline of hydrographic investigations in the Mediterranean; these would have included such observations as the ocean's behaviour, changes in the depth of water, the influence of currents, identifying unexpected rock formations and the movement of sediment. If ships were not to founder on rocks, be off course by virtue of undetected currents or stranded on sandbanks, all these probings were vital to an overall knowledge of navigation in general, and the importance of the work cannot be over-emphasised. There was also a secondary reason for keeping a presence in the enclosed waters of the Mediterranean. The disintegration of the Ottoman Empire meant that British interests needed to be quietly on the alert, and the very presence of benign warships sent a political message without any need for further action. This remains the case today and surface warships play an enormously important part in a peacekeeping role.

HARBOUR SERVICE LIST, 1895–1900

In 1895 *Gannet* was out of commission at Chatham for four months, before being taken back to her home port of Sheerness. By December 1895 she suffered the indignity of being transferred to the harbour service list. Worse was to come in the following year: in June 1896 she was transferred back to Chatham, where for the next four years she was put on the list of non-effective vessels. In mitigation for this ignominy, it does firmly establish her previous connections with Chatham Dockyard, but her presence at this time was a sad farewell to a bygone era. No one then would ever have predicted her glorious return a century later.

DIRE STRAITS

The shame of old age has been suffered by all four of the UK transitional ships in the latter stages of their lives before being rescued: SS *Great Britain* became a coal hulk at Port Stanley in the Falklands and later a depot for sheepskins in Sparrows' Cove, where she had been towed out to die in the late 1960s. She was by then 120 years old. Out of service, HMS *Warrior* was reduced to being hulk *C77* for fifty years as part of Pembroke Docks, until the late 1970s. She was also

nearly 120 years old; SS *Discovery* was so badly neglected after the part she had played in the First World War that she almost fell apart in Vosper's repair yard at Portsmouth in 1923 and was described as needing 'reconditioning and practically reconstructing for further service'.

Before returning to Dundee in 1979, *Discovery* was unrigged at her berth on the Thames Embankment, and all masts, the funnel and other topside gear removed, and she was towed down the river to Sheerness for repair and reconstruction, as one of the last jobs in which that shipyard was involved.

ACCOMMODATION HULK: SOUTH EASTERN & CHATHAM RAILWAY COMPANY, 1900–1902

October 1900 marked the lowest point of *Gannet's* life. She was listed as an accommodation hulk and leased to the South Eastern & Chatham Railway Company on the Isle of Grain. At this time there was a 'cross-channel' railway terminal at Port Victoria, which was not a success and the company withdrew from the initiative in 1901. This would have been a dangerous moment for *Gannet's* survival but a lucky break came with the Admiralty's need to relieve HMS *President*, the Royal Naval Reserve ship berthed in London's West India Docks. *Gannet* was renamed for the first time in her life: as HMS *President* she became the new headquarters for the RNVR and was converted into a drill ship.

DRILL SHIP, 1903–1911

In 1909 she was renamed as *President II*, but by the spring of 1911 she was replaced by another Sheerness-built composite vessel, HMS *Buzzard* (1887), and so once again was placed on the list of non-effective vessels. Once again, she had reached the lowest ebb.

RENAMED TS *MERCURY* 1913–1968

By 1913 the naval arms race between Britain and Germany had reached a point where war was seen as an inevitability, and young men were needed in abundance to man the new century's steel battleships, cruisers and destroyers. There would be no place in the impending war for wooden warships, but just a few of them would be required as shore-based training facilities.

THE TRAINING SCHOOL *MERCURY*

Charles A R Hoare was a gentleman who had in his younger days enjoyed life to the full, growing ever richer after a successful career in banking. He was a senior partner of Hoare's Bank in London, and described as being 'very rich indeed' in 1877. He and his wife Margaret had four sons and a daughter. In his later years he had philanthropically

7

HMS *President II*, ex-*Gannet*, in the Hamble. From a collection of photos held by the *Mercury* Old Boys' Association. (A L White)

established a training school with his own money, offering to take youngsters of age fourteen and upwards, some as young as eleven, off the streets of London and give them a chance to train for naval service. It was a noble venture.

With his considerable wealth he had built and designed a fine house at Binney's Hard, overlooking the River Hamble. He also owned a full-sized sailing barque named *Illovo* moored on the Hard, but which by the early years of the twentieth century was barely seaworthy.

His idea was that *Gannet*, renamed *President II*, could replace the ailing vessel *Illovo*, and adopt the name of the school as TS *Mercury*; the replacement vessel was slightly larger and could be used as a dormitory and drill ship, whilst lessons and meals would continue to be held in the classrooms of the shore-based house. These lessons were mainly concerned with what was necessary for turning young boys from their former lives on the streets of London into useful sailors. Music was encouraged as a subject and continued a tradition of providing the ship with a sizeable band. The boys also enjoyed the use of a 7in gauge live steam railway, whose track ran from the house to the shore line, a boyish enthusiasm of A R Hoare. He also had a fine historic collection of model ships kept in the house.

As *President II* remained on loan from the Admiralty when transferred into her new role, her maintenance was still their responsibility, but this was the only contribution

they made to the school. This maintenance programme is a small but vital detail to the long-term existence and preservation of *Gannet;* similarly this same regular RN diligence is the particular reason that *Warrior*'s hull also survives. These two ships' hulls have been consistently maintained and looked after, even at times in their long lives when they have had no effective RN status. As *Gannet* had already been converted into a drill hall as HMS *President* in London 1903, she was viewed favourably as a floating facility to replace *Illovo*, being in a more sound condition and with more usable space aboard than her predecessor. The stripped-out shell was ideally suited for conversion for dormitory accommodation, ship-craft and gun drill, using deck-mounted and central pivot guns, combined with muscular sports under the canopy of the roof space. A rigged mizzenmast was soon added to the roof structure, for exercises in seamanship and going aloft to man the yards. She now once again had a purposeful role, and a fresh location on the River Hamble, close by East Meon and moored offshore from the main school building belonging to Charles Hoare.

By 1908 Charles Hoare felt that he wanted to hand over his school to a younger man. On the face of it, this exchange of headship with the civilian C B Fry and his wife Beatie seemed to be an ideal choice. C B Fry had a nationally recognised, glittering sports career behind him, as well as having gained a reputation for distinguished academic achievement. Nevertheless, quite soon after the school was transferred into his care, the lack of applause and adoration for his sporting prowess, to which he had become addicted, affected him in a very negative way – the word 'backwater' was never more appropriately used. His enthusiasm for

8

Captains and managers of TS *Mercury*: Charles Hoare, the founder of TS *Mercury*, 1885–1908; C B Fry, director and marine superintendent (honorary RNR), 1908–1950; Beatrice Fry OBE, manager 1908–1946. (Courtesy A L White)

running the training school as captain superintendent with the honorary rank of commander RNR soon waned, whilst his wife Beatie Fry's role became ever more influential, promoting the school's training scheme with 'messianic ferocity'.

Maritally speaking this was a complicated situation. Despite her high-born status, in 1877, at the tender age of fifteen, Beatie (Sumner) had already become the mistress of Charles Hoare, the founder of the *Mercury* training school, and by whom she had had two illegitimate children, scandalous at that time. When their association eventually cooled, she came under the spell of the young and talented sportsman C B Fry, described in his earlier days as 'the handsomest man in England'. After an uneasy truce between the two men, and somewhat to the relief of Charles Hoare, her former lover, Beatie Sumner eventually married C B Fry on 4 June 1898. Her baby Charis was born in February 1899, eight months after the marriage, followed by Stephen in 1900 and Faith in 1910, by which time Beatie Fry was forty-eight years old. Despite being a mother of five children, for the *Mercury* boys now under her charge she established a harsh and even cruel regime. Everyone knows that attitudes were very different then, but any senior naval officer would have been sickened by the cruel treatment and often unnecessary punishments handed out to these disadvantaged children, and the regime is shocking to modern readers. Up to a maximum of 150 boys would regularly be lined up to

'witness punishment'. What they were then forced to see was one of their own number, who was first taken to the gymnasium, stripped naked before reappearing wearing a pair of thin white cotton trousers. The boy was then tied to a gun barrel if he could not take the punishment standing up, and sadistically flogged until the blood ran down his legs, almost always in the presence of Beatie Fry who looked on impassively, awarding up to a maximum of twelve strokes. She was able to increase this punishment to twenty-four strokes if she chose, but only to be administered on a separate day. Beatings of this kind were administered as punishment for as little as 'being a general nuisance'.

In their everyday routine, the boy seamen slept in hammocks all year round aboard the unheated ship, and in winter their bare feet had to cross the frost-laden decking and planked causeway to go ashore. For minor misdemeanours, a regular punishment was to send the offender up to the cross-trees 50ft above the ground, and stand there all day without food or water. Any lapse of concentration could lead to a fatal fall onto the roofing of the ship. This never happened, but in winter the boy could become so cold and frightened that other boys would have to climb the rigging and help him down. The younger boys' dormitory was sited in the ship's hold, whilst the elder boys occupied the upper drill hall. Perhaps most cruelly of all, the boys' individualism and personalities were stamped out of them by shaving their heads like convicts and referring to them simply by numbers and not by their names.

None of this detail would have been known or recorded, except that one of their number, Ronald Morris, later wrote and published a book called *The Captain's Lady* (1985). The 'lady' in question refers to Mrs Beatie Holme Fry, who was, ironically, awarded the OBE in the Birthday Honours list of King George V in 1918, for 'services to the war'. She received her award at Buckingham Palace a fortnight before

the war ended. The sad truth is that this system produced the precise results for which the Royal Navy and the Merchant Marine were looking. The boys from the *Mercury* Training School were exactly what was needed, particularly when so many more were required for the opening stages of

9

Physical training. (Courtesy A L White)

10

The dining hall. (Courtesy A L White)

Edited extracts from the ship's log

1879	17 April	Commissioned at Sheerness. Commander Edmund G Burke RN appointed as captain.
	26 May	Sailed from Portsmouth on her first commission employed on the Pacific Station (Panama) 1879–1883.
	30 June	Arrived at Rio de Janeiro, Brazil (via Funchal Bay, Madeira) where first leave granted to her crew.
	July–August	Sailed via Straits of Magellan to Valparaiso, Chile. Called at Possession Bay, South Georgia (to coal ship). Port Famine, Fortescue Bay, Port Chirrucca, Isthmus and Mayne Harbour.
	31 August	Arrived Valpairaiso. Leave granted.
	4 September	Sailed via Coquimbo, Iquique, Arica, Mollendo and Callao to Panama.
1880	27 June	Arrived Panama. Visited islands of Tobago, Sabago and Pedro Gonzales. Sailed for Honolulu, Hawaii.
	24 October	Arrived Honolulu. Sailed for the USA. Called at San Francisco and Acapulco.
1880/1		Sailed around the Pacific, calling at Hawaii, Hilo, Fannings Island, Christmas Island, Jarvis Island, Malden Island and Tahiti.
1881	7 January	Arrived Coquimbo.
	February	Underwent mid-commission refit at Esquimalt, Canada.
1881/2		Cruised the Pacific Ocean.
1883	28 April	Arrived at Montevideo, Uruguay on her return passage to the UK.
	27 June	Anchored off Plymouth breakwater.
	20 July	Paid off at Sheerness by the Port Flag Captain. Sailed approx 60,000 miles.
	21 July	Dismantled in steam basin at Sheerness, placed in 4th Division Medway Steam Reserve. Removed to Chatham Dockyard until required for further service.
1884	June	Refit at No. 2 Dock Sheerness.
1885	February	Fitted with electrical machinery for spar torpedoes. Fitted with long range 5in BL guns, replacing 32pdr ML guns.
	June	Completed for active service and placed on list of vessels ready for commission.
	3 September	Recommissioned at Sheerness to relieve HMS Bittern on the Mediterranean Station. Command of Commander Barton R Bradford RN.
	19 September	Sailed for Devonport.
	21 September	Arrived Devonport.
	25 September	Sailed for Station.
	10 October	Arrived Valletta Harbour, Malta.
	15 October	Sailed for Suakin via Port Said and Suez Canal.
	30 October	Arrived Suakin.
	November	Sailed between Khor Shinab, Mersa Halaib, boarded and captured dhows.
	5 December	Sailed for Suez.
	10 December	In dock at Suez for repairs (rudder damaged).
1886	21 January	Sailed for Suakin via Mersa Sheikh Barud.
	26 January	Arrived Suakin.
	28 January–19 March	Sailed Mersa Halaib, Mersa Sheikh Barud, Khor Shinab, Ras Benas, Mersa Abu Amara, Cape Elba, Maccorah Island and Suakin.
	7 April	Sailed for Trinikitat and Ras Assis. Boarded dhows.
1887	30 April	Lt W G Sewart RN killed while commanding one of Gannet's boats, in an exchange of fire with a suspected slaving dhow off Mersa Halaib, Sudan.
	2 May	Arrived Suakin. Governor General (Colonel Kitchener RE) ordered expedition to find and arrest the murderers.
1888	August–September	Undergoing mid-commission refit at Malta.
	11 September	Arrived Suakin relieved HMS Dolphin.

	17 September	Opened fire on Osman Digna's rebels, in support of land forces. Main armament fired 200 shells and Nordenfelt machine guns nearly 1,200 rounds over the 27 days involved in the defence of Suakin.
	15 October	Relieved by HM Ships *Racer* and *Starling*.
	1 November	Paid off at Malta.
	10 November	Recommissioned at Malta. Command of Commander H Corfe RN.
1888–92		Fleet support duties in the Eastern Mediterranean mainly on hydrographic surveys.
1895	16 March	Paid off at Chatham. Placed in 'C' Division Dockyard Reserve, Chatham. Moved to Sheerness Dockyard. Stripped of her boilers, engine, propeller shaft and funnel.
	December	Placed on list of ships available for harbour service.
1896	June	Returned to Chatham.
1900	2 May	Placed on list of non-effective vessels. Lent to the South Eastern & Chatham Railway as an accommodation hulk at Port Victoria, Isle of Grain, Kent, UK.
1902	June	Completed service as an accommodation hulk
1902/3		Conversion to drill ship. Support pillars on existing deck beams for the new upper drill hall installed. Continuous centre line girder from fo'c'sle to poop deck. Gun recesses planked over. Sash windows installed.
1903	31 March	Entered service as HQ Ship Royal Naval Volunteer Reserve, at West India Docks, London.
	16 May	Renamed *President*.
1909		Re-named *President II*.
1911		Replaced by HMS *Buzzard* as HQ Ship RNR. Placed on list of non-effective vessels available for subsidiary purposes.
1913	October	Lent to Mr C B Fry and renamed TS *Mercury*. Converted into an accommodation ship at Sheerness. Transferred to the River Hamble near Southampton.
1968	15 July	TS *Mercury* School closed. Ship returned to the Royal Navy.
1971		Acquired by The Maritime Trust
1987		Arrived at Chatham for restoration under charter from The Maritime Trust.
1993	October	New 69ft foremast stepped.
1994	February	New 29ft bowsprit.
	October	New 58ft mizzenmast.
1996		Purchased by Chatham Historic Dockyard Trust.

the First World War, and those *Mercury* boys who had survived the course were actively sought after by recruiting officers, who knew that not only was their training thorough, but that these boys would go on to teach others who had been less thoroughly instructed. The school was much improved at the end of Beatie Fry's regime under a new superintendent, Commander M S Bradby, and continued right through the Second World War, finally to be closed down in 1968.

Once again, *Gannet*'s usefulness had come to an end, but her luck held, because this was a time when the British nation was waking up to the issue of preserving, rather than destroying, these old nineteenth-century vessels. Three years later, in 1971, the ownership of *Gannet/Mercury* officially transferred to the recently formed Maritime Trust founded in 1970, which then became responsible for her restoration and preservation, transferring her ownership for the first time from the Royal Navy into civilian care under the auspices of The Maritime Trust.

THE IN-BETWEEN YEARS, 1968–2000

Gannet's journey to Chatham was to be a slow one. After a survey in Southampton she was towed to Gosport to be moored close to Priddy's Hard in Fareham Creek. Then in 1978 some volunteers made a start on restoration work and in 1983 the HMS *Gannet* (1878) Society was helped by Royal Navy volunteers from *Daedalus*, *Sultan* and *Collingwood*. However, funds were limited and difficulties were exacerbated by the offshore mooring so workers and materials could only access the vessel by boat – money and a dry dock were desperately required. Although initial hopes for a berth at Powder Pier, near the Armaments Museum, as part of Priddy's Hard Heritage site, were to be dashed when the museum was closed and the site earmarked for development, another solution emerged and Chatham Historic Dockyard took on the conservation and restoration of the ship.

As *Gannet* left Portsmouth, so *Warrior* arrived; the very same towing team took *Gannet* on her way home to the

11

<small>HMS</small> *Gannet*, now under cover in preparation for restoration, 16 August 2002. (Nielsen archive)

12

The reality of ship restoration: replacing a line of rivets in the bilge, 30 August 2002. (Nielsen archive)

Medway, where she arrived on 18 June 1987. The Royal Navy had left Chatham in 1984, handing over responsibility for the site to the Chatham Historic Dockyard.

The restoration project was overseen by staff at Chatham, together with a committee of trustees. The work was undertaken by T Nielsen & Co Ltd of Gloucester, specialists in the repair and restoration of traditional ships, under the direction of naval architect Fred M Walker with BMT Ship Design, and the workforce was recruited through a local community work programme.

Five to seven years was the time estimate for completion, and the work was actually completed 'on time and on budget', a testament to the excellent working relationship to

13

The hull stripped out: a mammoth task lies ahead, 13 August 2002. (Nielsen archive)

be found in the whole restoration team from architect to constructor.

The first step was to clear debris and ballast from the ship – 57 tons of pig iron comprised the latter, and the debris was also measured in tons. This was followed by draining the dock to allow a full inspection and assessment of the state of the ship. The enormity of the task was gradually revealed. Although the wrought iron frames and upper deck beams were sound, much had been removed, including iron bulkheads, carlings, beams and deck planking. The former bunkers, engine, boiler and condenser rooms were an empty shell.

In 1902 the fo'c'sle had been modified and in the process the original recessed gun ports were stripped out, with extra frames and planks being fitted. However, when the restorers removed these, the steel and iron plating under the deck planking was so corroded that it necessitated a complete rebuild of this area.

There were other major works too: the only surviving original features in the inboard hull were storage bins, cabinets and other fixtures in the forward hold. The considerable modifications made over the years had, in effect, gutted this area of the ship. But there were bonuses, as well: under the copper sheathing of the hull, much of the planking was not in a bad condition. The worst areas of rot were to be found in the stern planking above upper deck level, the stem timbers and the two false keels. A similar situation was to be found on the poop deck.

Once again, the modifications over the years had also left their mark on the upper deck: although some of the original planking was extant, so many original features such as hatches, skylights, etc, had been taken out and large access ways added in, that a complete replanking of the deck was required.

14

Close inspection of the stern-post and propeller well, 11 September 2002. (Nielsen archive)

15

Arc-welding the uprights on the portside of the poop decking, 31 October 2002. (Nielsen archive)

this training scheme, but local and county council funding enabled the maintenance of a small core of workers. The National Heritage Memorial Fund also funded some of the conservation aspects of the project, particularly copper sheathing and painting. As Duncan Cochrane writes, 'In everything that we did and continue to do, the broad aim was to carry out the work as authentically as possible by employing the materials and methods that were used in the original construction.'

So, in essence, *Gannet* would have to be rebuilt, apart from the hull and framing. Grit-blasting and coating the original ironwork with red lead was the first step, in order to halt any corrosion, and the hull planking was painted.

Progress on the restoration was not all smooth. When the government replaced the community work programme with employment training, with its focus on the gaining of qualifications rather than the providing of work for the unemployed, participants ended up in the workshop rather than on the ship. Government then withdrew funding from

16

Setting up the sheds and workshop at Chatham, 5 September 2002. (Nielsen archive)

2: Making a Start: The Hull

17

In the workshop. Just as Nielsens needed to set up workshops at Chatham Dockyard, it is important to attend to the details of the workshop before construction of the model ship can begin. This photograph shows the bench top under construction. I need to make a table-top which is carefully constructed to be accurately square and also adjustable for levelling, so that it is perfectly horizontal – to the point where I can use a spirit level with confidence to check the progress with items like mast housings and deck levels. It also enables the accurate use of a surface gauge, a most useful measuring tool from the world of engineering. It is vital that this table-top can be easily clamped from all sides and that it is the correct height.

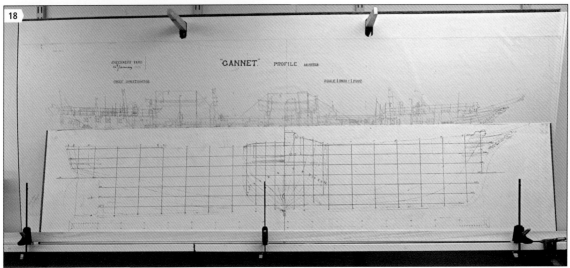

18

The profile and body lines of *Gannet*, redrafted from the available plans from the National Maritime Museum, London, by Malcolm Darch, a FSNR professional model shipwright. Note the use of shelf racking for the display of plans. The National Maritime Museum has copies of *Gannet's* profile plan, upper deck, lower deck, hold, etc, but the non-availability of a lines and body plan was the vital missing link, without which it was not possible to make a start. There are very few people left in the UK who still have Malcolm's skill in draughtsmanship, where ships' lines are drawn from scratch, and it is a skill which simply distinguishes the amateur from the professional. Five separate ply-boards were used to suspend the plans from wall brackets for easy access. Unless a ship's plans are readily accessible, one can spend a great deal of

precious time trying to locate details. Furling and unfurling rolled plans is not really very practical, either, when trying to measure an item accurately. Having said that, it is very handy to have a second rolled copy, for the purposes of photocopying detail later on in the build: once ship's plans are either pasted down or stuck down to a board, this possibility is no longer an option, so two sets are really essential. Note also that if you are pasting plans down with wallpaper paste, the image will expand by approximately 2 per cent, and allowance must be made for this, or there will be a lot of mismatching. To avoid this, there are several paper spray mount products which act on the paper without any stretch factor, but get assistance from another pair of hands when laying them down, or you could well find yourself in an expensive and sticky mess.

ADMIRALTY SPECIFICATIONS 1874

Numbered 1–221, these were the contractual orders issued by the Admiralty for the building of the Cormorant class of vessel and contain all the details for the work to be undertaken in the shipyard, legally defining the responsibilities of both parties.

No. 1

The hull of the ship is to be built, fitted, and made complete in all respects (with the exceptions hereinafter stated), with cabins, mess rooms and store rooms of every description, magazines, shell rooms, and light boxes, and with all drainage, pumping and ventilating arrangements, as hereafter described in this specification, by the official drawings, and the sketches

hereafter to be made, and in accordance with the directions of the Overseer.

No. 8

Keel to be of English elm faced with teak where it is in contact with the flat keel plate and worked as on the midship section; to be well secured to the flat keel-plate, and staple angle irons with copper bolts, well clenched on metal rings.

No. 9

False keels to be of English elm 12 inches wide and 4 inches thick, worked as shown on the midship section, and fastened with metal dumps [a dump is a large cylindrical nail and a short bolt combined].

19

19

Stationing the frames: the radial arm saw, poised and ready for cutting the slots into the keel. It is easy to sigh with a note of envy when you see a machine which is perfectly suited to the job in hand, and the DeWalt radial arm saw, despite its great age (bought in 1967), is a wonderful aid to accurate slot-cutting, and a good deal else, as well. I hasten to add that this procedure can be done by hand, because I have done it with a tenon saw and a fine chisel in the past, but that is obviously a longer journey. The width/kerf of the TCT circular saw-blade has to be carefully adjusted at the point of entry, but the job is quickly done, with matched grooves on either side. It is also possible to do this job with a miniature router.

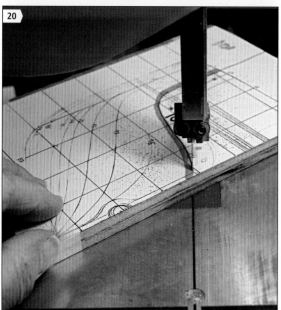

20

ADMIRALTY SPECIFICATION No. 18, TRANSVERSE FRAMES

The transverse frames are to be 19 inches apart, from centre to centre from 41 station forward and 20 inches apart abaft 41 station ... the butts of the reverse angle irons are to be properly shifted and are to be covered by angle iron butt straps ... the floor plates, of which the frames are partly composed, are to be either welded or butt-strapped together, the welds or butts giving good shift with the butts of the reverse angle irons.

20

Cutting out the bulkhead frames. The frames are dowelled together and then taped as a pair for machining, so that when they are opened up, they exactly match one another. This is referred to as 'book-leafing'.

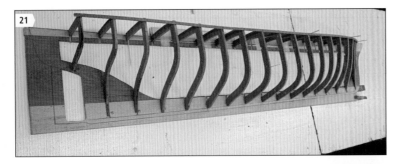

Bulkhead frames set port and starboard. The top of the keel-piece has been removed, and adjusting tongues at the top of the frames allow for the tiny gap where the frames join at the top. The ability to fractionally adjust the alignment of the bulkheads is useful. The propeller shaft tubing is also fitted at this early stage.

21

Keel-piece with bulkhead frames attached. It is vital at this stage to ensure the frames are set squarely into the slots and that a flexible length of timber can test the fairness of the frames. It is almost certain that small adjustments will need to be made at this point. The starboard side is laid up first with backbone strength given to the keel by the plywood, particularly at the stern-post, around the area of the propeller aperture. In full scale, it also shows that the keel is deepened at the stern in comparison with the stem, for the increased advantage gained by *Gannet* being designed primarily as a sailing ship, rather than a steamer. Note also the extra grip given to the keel by not trimming it off at this early stage. This extra depth is intentionally left in place, so that it can be easily gripped by the aluminium angle pieces fixed to the building board.

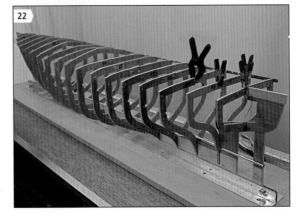

23

Sketch of plank-bender. The first requirement for executing the challenging task of the rounded stern is some sort of jig for warming up a 2in copper tube, around which the planks will be persuaded to take the necessary curvature. Mine is a lash-up, refreshingly crude in construction, and just in case anyone else wants to make one of a similar design, I include a sketch of the device.

24

Gas-powered plank-bender. Timber strip for planking needs to be soaked before it is made to bend over a hot 2in copper tube; the time of the soak is really 'the longer the better', but half an hour will be sufficient to take the curvature on the stern of this particular model. The strip is 1/4 x 1/16in Brazilian mahogany. The hand-held blowlamp is fired up by butane, set on a low light, and this will warm up the copper tube within a minute. The unit needs to be clamped to a bench for safety – keep your wrist away from the hot end. The idea is that the copper tube acts as a gently heated former, over which wet planks are laid, with pressure applied. When dried out, they will hold the new shape.

25

Bringing pressure to bear. *Gannet* restoration programme at Chatham Dockyard (from the Nielsen archive, 16 January 2003). Essentially, Nielsen's process is exactly the same for plank-bending as mine. Their timber is first placed in a long enclosed steam-chest, and whilst still soaking hot and wet from steam pressure, it is taken straight to the metal former and bent over the curvature of the framing; the shape of the planking is taken from precise measurements and patterns previously lifted from the hull. On account of the thickness of the stern planking, a pulley and winch become involved, and the plank is clamped to the steel former as the bending takes place. It is then quickly bolted onto the upright frames of the poop deck whilst still pliable. In the picture it is a straight plank being formed; where bevel angle is also required (see below), wooden wedges are included on the metal former to give both bend and twist. This job is not without danger, but follows the ancient practice of shipwrights using the steamed plank-on-frame technique.

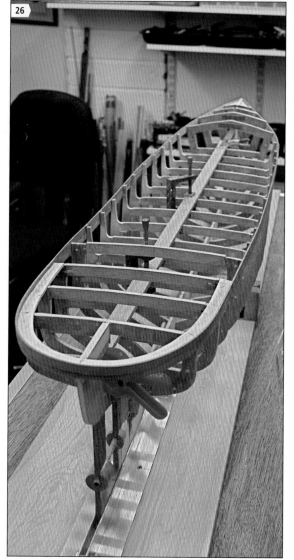

ADMIRALTY SPECIFICATION No. 15, SHAFT TUBE

The tube to receive the propeller shaft is to be prepared fitted and turned out by the Shipbuilder; to be 7/8ths inch thick the joint being covered by an edge strip of the same thickness. This tube is to be securely attached to the post and to the stuffing-box bulkhead and built into the frames of the ship which are to be bossed out in a suitable form for the purpose. The whole work is to be done to the entire satisfaction of the Overseer.

No. 10
The stem is to be a combination of iron and wood … the upper pieces of the wood portion are to be of English oak, the piece in contact with the iron stem is to be faced with teak; the lower pieces are to be of English oak or elm, moulded as per drawing and sided at the fore part of fore rabbet 10 inches at the head and 9 inches at the heel.

26

The model hull takes shape. With the gunwale in place and the elliptical stern planked round, a centre line is established with a straight edge clamped to the full length of the hull. All these early measurements are vital to the final accuracy of the hull. A 'stagger' has to be cut into the supporting upright of the stern overhang, looking somewhat like the sweep of a staircase, and the 'steps' should have been cut to allow for a double thickness of planks at this point. I have just about got away with a single step, but have had to reinforce the inside where the horizontal joins are perilously thin. A filler or stopper could have been used, but I wanted to avoid that if possible.

27

Poop deck plank. In this picture of the full-size restoration (Nielsen archive, 6 February 2003), not only has this thick section of planking been steamed and bent into shape, it also has a bevel angle on it, imparted by the insertion of wedges into the steel former. Once formed, the plank will be bolted to the upright steel frames as soon as possible.

30

In-filled plank. The metal scriber points to the in-filled plank; this has been fashioned with the spoke-shave on one side only, and marked with a small pencil 'V' on the trimmed side; it is then fitted into the swell, whilst the flat side of the plank is laid facing towards the keel. Both sides of the plank are glued and then 'spiled' in. The glue acts as a lubricant and by feeding the trimmed plank in carefully, the gap will be filled invisibly. Do not trim the blunt end until it has been pushed home; the 45-degree adjoining cut can then be made over the bulkhead, for the next plank to be laid against and joined.

28

The rabbet. A chisel is being used to deepen the rebate which runs all the way round the stem, keel and stern-post; this view is of the upturned stem-piece at the base of the clipper bow. Note that the first plank, known as the garboard strake, has already been laid against the keel, sitting snugly in the rebate. The model planking is made from best quality Brazilian mahogany strip.

29

A round-faced spoke-shave is an essential tool for planking model ships. Because of its rounded face, the exposed blade can cope with making a long, thin, scalloped section on the edge of a plank. This process requires a miniature shooting board, which is a simple enough jig to make, where two sheets of 1/8in aluminium come together to grip the pair of planks as they are planed down as a pair. This process will produce long, thin tongues, which can be pushed into the narrow gap demanded by the ever-changing shape of a model ship's hull. No other hand tool (or machine) can achieve this hollowed-out shape, applied to only one side of the plank. The spoke-shave is a difficult tool to use at first, but with a really sharp blade, it is guaranteed to produce a smile of satisfaction as the miniature planks are reduced to a whisper at their ends. The spoke-shave shown is made by Lie Nielsen, USA, and is predictably expensive.

ADMIRALTY SPECIFICATION NO. 14

Bilge keels to be each about 70ft long, the inner piece to be of teak and the outer pieces of English elm to be scored over the frames to the depth of one and a half inches and worked between two angle irons … the butts of these angle irons are to be well secured by covering angle irons of the same size, so that they may be efficiently welded together … the bilge keels are to be secured to the frames with mixed metal screws 3/4in diameter, tapped into the frames and having nuts on their points … the intersection of the plane of the bilge keels with the middle longitudinal plane is to be parallel to the water-line.

31

Restoration of the stern. Here *Gannet* is in the graving dock at Chatham, resting on the keel blocks and shored up; this Nielsen photo was taken on 3 September 2003 with all the coppering secured. The process of plating began in early March 2003 and was completed on 16 September the same year.

32

Bilge plank. With the model it is essential to establish the line of the bilge keels, and lay the bilge plank down as a marker. This allows for a controlled expansion on both sides of the hull working towards this fixed point. Never be tempted to plank one side of the hull first, because it will distort the hull's shape; always progress with matched planks on both sides of the hull.

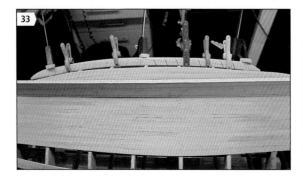

33

Starboard bilge keel being fitted. Stress-relieving saw-cuts allow for the curvature of this keel, in full scale 73ft. Owing to the relatively shallow hull of a gun vessel, these steadying keels play an important part in their stability.

35

Tailoring the stern. The planking surrounding the stern requires individual attention. Certain planks also require steaming on the plank bender, and a constant use of the spoke-shave to ensure a close fit. The design of the rounded stern of this ship gives this vessel not only a degree of elegance, but also good sea-keeping qualities in a following sea. The stern would rise in a 'pooping' sea and keep the quarterdeck from becoming awash in all but the very worst weather. This design was much favoured by Scottish-built whalers and polar vessels for this very reason, and *Gannet* was designed as a ship which might be called to the furthest reaches of the British Empire, and had to be suited to all weather conditions.

37

Clipper bow. Any ship's hull with this feature announces the halcyon days of sail. Note that the model still retains the false keel.

34

Upright hull of the model. Planking is now well advanced and shows the sheer of the vessel to good advantage. The soft sweep of the gunwale is immediately visible now that the hull is the right way up, with an appreciable sheer to the upper planking, satisfyingly echoing the line of the bilge keel. You can now see very clearly that this hull is designed for easy passage through the water.

36

Closing the planking of the stern. Sanding off the contours of the rounded stern with a hand-held, homemade sanding bobbin, simply a sanding sheet wrapped around some polystyrene pipe insulation, joined with drafting tape.

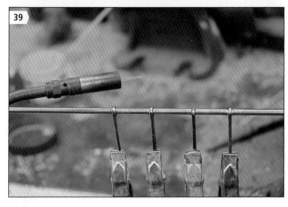

38

Glass-fibre gelcoat. This is neat resin applied to the interior to stabilise the wooden hull by the skilled hands of Steve Taylor. Gelcoat is the outer layer used in the lay-up of glass reinforced polyester lamination (GRP), a process normally associated with mould-making. When the two-part mix of gelcoat has been mixed, it combines to give a very hard but slightly flexible surface, which is ideal for sealing up all those little joints and expansion cracks which any newly built wooden hull will possess and, at the same time, strengthening the hull as a total monocoque structure. It is, of course, taking the place of the old-fashioned and arduous job of caulking with 'tar and small stuff' in full-scale wooden boatbuilding. The mixture has a thixotropic (jelly-like) component which makes it very suitable for application to seal up the almost inaccessible places at the stem and stern of the vessel, without 'runs', and it can be poured into these places by gravity feed if necessary, or by injection with a syringe. Its ability to seal out water ingress is legendary, but it must be carefully applied if it is being used as a base for the glassfibre mat strand which is to be subsequently laid over it, when it has cured off.

39

Pintle straps for the rudder. For the model, these are narrow strips of brass, wrapped around brass tube, using gravity via the clips to be soft-soldered with an open flame. This is technically known as a sweated joint and is superior to one made with a soldering iron, because the heat opens up the metal surface by expansion, accepting the solder into the surface. Water-soluble solder flux is used.

40

Pintle straps are glued into a sawn groove across the rudder, holding the soldered brass tube in place, and aligned. When the glue has fully set, the tubing is cut away, leaving only a bearing tube into which the aligned pins can be soldered.

41

Shipping and unshipping the rudder. The rudder is removable as in SS *Discovery*. The rudder post straps are made in the same way as those on the rudder stock and the pintle slots are known as the 'gulleting'. The model timber is wenge, which always has an aged look to it, even when newly sawn.

42

43

Rudder sole-piece and staples. With the old copper cladding removed, the excellent condition of the double-planked Burmese teak of the original is fully displayed in this Nielsen photograph from 18 July 2002. The bronze fittings which support this vulnerable part of the ship include the sole-plate and the upright supporting staples and pintle straps. The caulking of the dumps is very evident. The wooden plug in the propeller shaft was most likely put into position when the vessel's engine and other fittings were removed in 1895.

Rudder fittings. The brass sole-piece and staples loosely assembled with clips. The staples are the horseshoe-shaped side reinforcements set up from the sole-plate, giving added strength to the rudder-post.

44

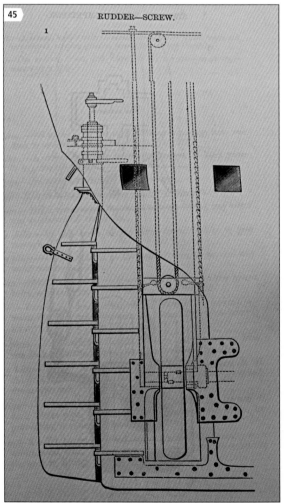

45

False keel removal. A coping saw is used for the removal of the false keel, leaving approximately one-third in the central portion of the model hull, in order that it can continue to be gripped by the aluminium angle section bolted to the baseboard.

45

Lifting propeller. The hoisting mechanism for a lifting propeller of this period is detailed in Sir George Nare's *Seamanship* manual (VIIth edition). Note that the reinforcing measures taken around the sole-piece and rudder-post in the illustration match those found on *Gannet*.

46

Installing the propeller well. The trunk of the well has a 4-degree negative rake to allow for the slope of the propeller shaft with which it must connect via the guides. The original installation of the propshaft had no universal coupling of any kind and was connected directly to the thrust block.

47

Restoration progress. In this picture (Nielsen archive, 17 June 2003), work is being carried out to the metal bulwarks, the hoops of the hammock racking, and renewal of the weather deck planking; the funnel base is in position and the coaming of a main hatchway sited.

48

Frames. This revealing picture from the Nielsen archive shows the state of the most vulnerable quarter of the hull/bilge – under the stoke-hold; it must have been almost impossible to keep a maintenance programme going with the difficulties of accessing this area during the time when boilers were fitted, but it is a tribute to her builders in Sheerness Dockyard that their work has endured for over 140 years. The problem for restorers is that if you start to remove one frame, a cascade of issues will follow. Sufficient to say that the rot has been arrested, the hull has been made watertight, and the vessel no longer has to endure the racking forces of a working hull.

49

Embrasure hinges. Working model hinge for the starboard embrasure. In full size, when the flap was lowered, it allowed the gun barrel to protrude through the port. The two side windows remained partially closed, giving some protection for the gun crew. I believe that working hinges add greatly to the success of any model, and are always worth the extra effort of fitting.

50

HMS *Gannet* **restoration.** Interior shot of the embrasure on the port-side from the Nielsen archive, 31 October 2002.

51

Anchor chocks (full-size) at the head of *Gannet,* finished in yellow ochre paint. Note the cutaway of the deck planking above the embrasures. This is to provide uninterrupted forward fire to the 64pdr bow-chaser gun housed below, a design feature only made possible by the extra strength given to iron-framed vessels.

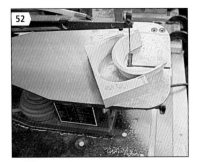

52

Anchor chocks (model). The scroll saw-table is set at 16 degrees for the first outer pass, then increased to 25 degrees for the second inner saw-cut, making the timber section thicker at the base than the top. The timber is English limewood.

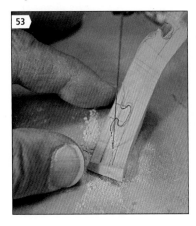

53

Fairlead slots of the anchor chocks, being fretted out with a powered piercing blade.

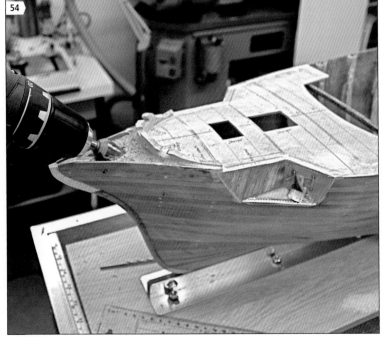

54

Bowsprit housing. Using a stepped cone drill to make way for housing the bowsprit. These drills are engineered not to snatch when multiple materials are involved, as in this case, where plywood, glassfibre mat and deck beams all meet. Cone drills were originally developed for drilling through sheet metal, at which they are very successful, and they have many other virtues as well. Note also the completed modelling of the port side armoured embrasure, with working hinges.

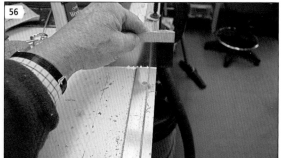

55

Moulding scraper steel (for model rails and brackets). Profiles for different shapes of mouldings can most easily be made from the flat edge of a cabinet scraper steel. A steel cutting disc (Dremel) is mounted in a slow-running chuck and can, with a little practice, make the profile shape required. Safety glasses and a mask must be worn because this work is hand-held and done by eye. *Warning* – some of these discs can and do fracture. The width of the pattern cut in the steel must match the width of the strip of timber being made.

56

Cabinet scraper steel in action. The scraper steel with the profile of the required pattern is gently moved to and fro along a length of timber strip, anchored at either end, and placed on a flat surface. With a stroking action in either push or pull form, the hardwood strip will quite quickly acquire the shape of the profile. It is very satisfying to see its progress! The photo shows the procedure, but is slightly confused by the reflection on the scraper itself.

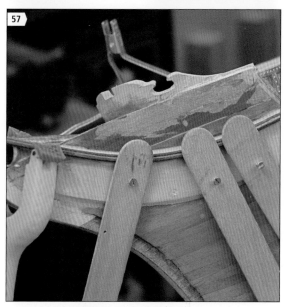

57

Trailboard moulding. The surround of the trailboard uses the first moulding strip. Note the remote clamping system using the ever-useful spatula sticks

58

Hair bracket mouldings on the restored *Gannet*, leading back from the figurehead to the twin anchor hawses set into the trailboard.

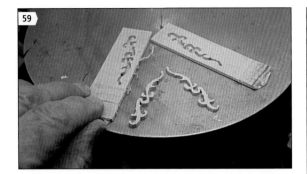

59

Trailboard detail. A thin strip of maple wood is first taped over on both sides. The pattern is marked out on one side, and fretted out with a piercing blade. The maple piece is then bandsawn in half and the two internal patterns, when released, will match perfectly.

ADMIRALTY SPECIFICATIONS NOS. 66 AND 67, SHIP'S HEADSHAFT TUBE

The ship's head is to be as shown upon the drawings, the planking running forward to form a clipper bow. The head is to be completed with cheeks, rails, berthing, figure(head), all necessary carved work, bolsters, straps for gammoning in accordance with the directions of the overseer.

No. 67
Quarter badges are to be fitted complete with all mock sashes, mouldings, carved work, etches, as is usual in HM service. Head and stern ornaments to be fitted complete in accordance with designs to be furnished or approved by the Controller of the Navy.

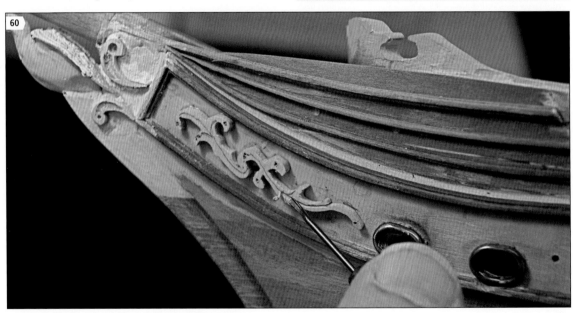

60

This scroll leaf pattern is conjectural, but fairly typical. No such carving exists on the restoration, but originally there was some, as shown on the ship's plans. The model work shows a 1.5mm 'V' gouge at work on the foliate scrolls. Interlinked with the trailboards are the anchor hawse outlets, with their double flared nostrils. They are set strangely low on the bottom rail of the trailboard's lower edge and have a linking piece to make them virtually all one casting. Hawse outlets are not round, but require 'squashing' to turn them into the correct shape; this is done using small-diameter copper piping; the trick is to slightly oversize the outlet's bore with the plain end of a twist drill bit, used as a dolly, before compressing them in the jaws of a vice. Once the rings are closed, they are then cleaned up

to rid them of the flux, lightly filed off on the aft side, making a flat area for the adhesive to grip, using GRP paste, which adheres admirably to copper. Late-nineteenth-century wood-carving was as much a part of shipbuilding as it was a part of Victorian England's housebuilding programmes. Any excuse, and the carving gouges and mallets came out to adorn and beautify solid blocks of timber.

Trailboards on larger ships were originally extra rubbing strakes at the ship's head, to try and prevent injury to a vulnerable part of the ship, but they ended up as feasts of decoration and ornamentation, sometimes with the details expensively gilded, in enhancement of the figurehead from which, visually, they always trailed aft.

61

The *Gannet* model figurehead. The body and wings have been fabricated from flat brass sheet, which gives the opportunity to mould the wings and provide a truly aggressive-looking neck. Softened brass shim, of which this basic shape is made, allows for beating metal over an anvil or former to make all sorts of shapes; it is much easier using metal and paste than carving such difficult items as wings. It also gives the opportunity to experiment with shape, which is another advantage of using metal rather than timber. On this model, Milliput resin putty is added to the body shape to fatten the bird and make it look less like a weather vane. Resin putty is a marvellous medium for modelmakers – at first totally malleable and miscible, it will adhere to almost any surface, and finally sets as hard as stone.

62

First coat of paint (model). The contrast which white paint gives shows off the carved work to the ship's head in a dramatic way. It also shows up every possible blemish imaginable. It was a big mistake to spray the lower half of the hull as well, much of which had to be scraped off.

3: Coppering

Copper cladding the hull in the days of ships with 'wooden walls' was all about keeping the ever-present *Teredo navalis* worm at bay; this was originally a tropical wood-boring weevil with the ability to make a quarter-inch hole right the way through a ship's hull in a short space of time. With the spread of infected hulls, it moved easily into European waters and became an international pest. Copper sheathing also prevented the bottoms of ships' hulls from becoming fouled up with kelp barnacles and weed, and the extra speed it gave to a warship was an obvious advantage. I am no gardener, but I understand plant life is not over-fond of copper. With copper plating on a ship's hull it is inaccurate to show any kind of protruding rivet/nail head, because the plates were flush-nailed to the hull, cushioned with a backing of tarred felt. So it was a smooth surface that was presented along the wetted area of the hull, with indentations here and there, where the hammering was over-enthusiastic. According to G F Campbell:

> Traditionally copper sheets were 48in in length x 14in to 20in in width according to the size of the hull, with pre-punched holes using a wood or metal jig. The leading edge and the top edge were left un-punched and inserted under the pre-punched but un-nailed edges of the previous plate. Nailing starts in the middle of the plate and works outwards to the corners with the edges secured last. The overlapped edges are hammered hard until hand-smooth.

Copper plating in model form requires the setting up of two home-made jigs. The first plating jig is aluminium angle, set onto a strip of plywood, with various widths of flat strip to be laid against it, so that a tailor's impressing wheel can be used to make the nail impressions required. These impressions point

inwards (the opposite of riveting, which requires the impressions to be outward facing). It is also necessary to have more than one impressing wheel with different pitches, as the nails in the middle of the copper plate are more sparsely pitched than those on the edges.

ADMIRALTY SPECIFICATIONS No. 215, COPPER SHEATHING

The copper will be supplied and put on by the Government, except on the keel and the false keel, between the keel and false keel, and three strakes on each side of the keel, copper on the forefoot, stem, stern-post and rudder, and under the metal casting at the heel of the stern-post, Kingston's valves etc. which must be put on whilst the ship is on the Contractor's premises, and at his expense – the necessary copper and nails being supplied by the Government, but the tarred paper by the Contractor; observing that the copper on front of stem, extending to at least 10ft abaft the fore foot to be 60oz per square foot, properly turned up and fastened. –The Contractor is also to cut out and fix all the necessary marks for the draught of water on both the stem and the stern post. Great care is to be taken to see that preparation is to be made to prevent any metallic connection between the copper sheathing and the iron frames of the ship, either through the propeller shaft, Kingston's, or other valves, lightning conductors, bolts, etc.

63

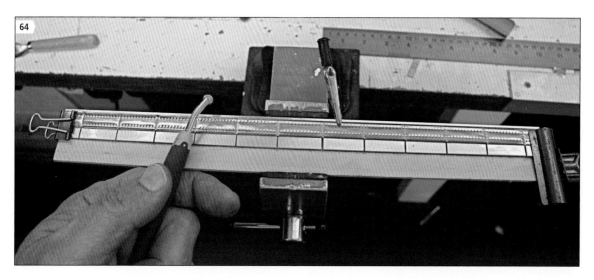

64

Second plating jig. This allows for the vertical joints of the plate to be accurately made, and consists of an aluminium strip with scored vertical lines marking the plate lengths. These 90-degree joints are immensely important to the final result; if they are out of alignment, it shows, and some hand-laid copper-clad models fail because of this detail. The small impressing tool here is by Pergamano.

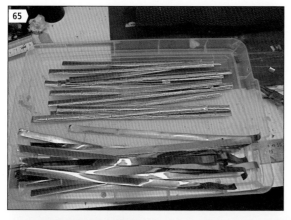

65

Guillotine. The ship's hull is clad with over 1,200 copper plates; if you can acquire an old chop guillotine, as used by photographers, and capable of cutting thick card, it helps enormously, but however it is done, the plate widths need to be fashioned with care and accuracy. Use a GRP paste for their fixing; it not only adheres well, but fills the gaps and cracks which inevitably appear in places. Thin strips of copper are difficult to handle, so the next jig involves a length of copper pipe, set up between two engineer's 'V' blocks; by giving the copper strip a little curvature, smoothed out with a half-round section of hardwood, sawn on the inside face to match the pipe's diameter, the strip can be made into a rigid and slightly concave section, which is easier to line up against a straight edge and provides a hollow into which GRP paste can be spread.

66

Nail impressions. The last job is to turn the impressions inwards rather than outwards, and this is easily done by reintroducing the strake to the copper tube and stroking it into shape with the wooden block, reversing the impressions into flattened holes, as is correct. The curvature/camber is also useful for loading the adhesive GRP paste when it comes to laying the strips of plating onto the hull. This is the moment for trimming off the ends with scissors.

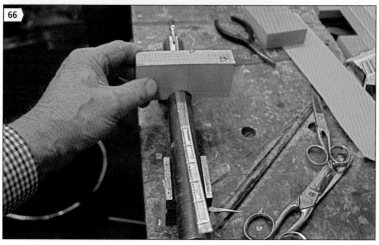

67

Copper plating the hull of HMS ***Gannet***: the enormous and costly task of coppering a full-sized hull (from the Nielsen archive, 12 March 2003). Note how the plates are correctly lapped, always starting from the stern, following the white lines and impressed with copper nailing holes.

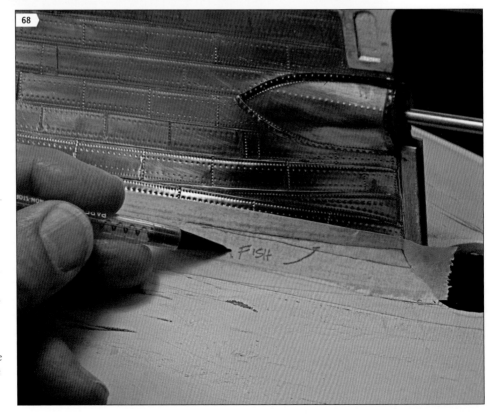

68

Propeller boss and stern coppering (model). The particular detail in this picture is fitting a fish-piece. There are several instances where this is necessary practice, as may be seen in the picture of the *Gannet* restoration above.

69

Identical issue in full scale. This Nielsen picture was taken on 13 May 2003, showing the need for the insertion of fish-plating. Note also that the interior of the propeller well is also clad with copper.

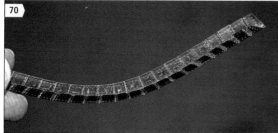

70

The wrapper plate for cladding the clipper bow (model). Bandsawn incisions have been made to allow for the curvature, almost to the centre line of the capping strip; owing to fact that the copper strip is annealed and is very soft, it is attached to plywood before the saw-cuts are made; this is to prevent snatching and bending. Copper is a very sticky metal, and not easy to cut, but it has so many other virtues; engineers refer to it as 'forgiving'.

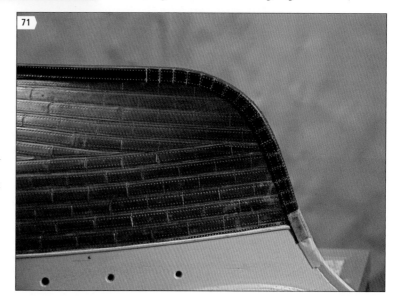

71

Wrapper plate as applied to the stem of the inverted model hull. Note also in this picture the joint line where the copper plates from the upper hull meet those of the lower hull – this is known as the 'goring band'. If the plates do not have precise vertical joints (see the second plating jig above), this is where it will show.

72

The greening effect of verdigris on the coppered hull is a simple wipe-on technique using a proprietary wax available from Liberon. The plating of the hull is prepared by scouring with wire wool, followed by an application of a weak solution of ferric chloride. This is necessary because the copper shim has a protective surface on the manufactured sheet of metal. This needs to be made dull before the

application of the wax. The vertical streaks are made with white spirits, which is a solvent for the wax product.

73

The graceful shape of the externally finished model hull from the fore quarter.

74

Completed plating to the model hull, stern view. Note the fine ink line denoting the water level; the bilge keel is also coppered.

75

Nielsen's dockyard workforce at Chatham, with the coppering of the ship completed (from the Nielsen archive, 16 September 2003).

4: Engines and Boilers

76

Humphrys & Tennant (Deptford) horizontal compound steam engine and boiler arrangements aboard *Gannet*, perspective view (done while a student in 1992 by Richard Chasemore and reproduced with his kind permission). I was faced with an historical problem: I knew who made the engine (Humphrys, Tennant & Co, Deptford, UK), and I knew the design of engine which was fitted. It was a horizontal compound steam engine rated at 1,100ihp, with one low- and one high-pressure cylinder fed from a massive steam pipe supplied in triplicate by the main boilers forward, but there are no original drawings, to my knowledge, of this particular engine, unlike the boilers, which are helpfully illustrated in elevation and plan view. As to the size of the engine, there is a very important clue given on the official lower-deck plans of the ship. The crankshaft is illustrated, which meant that I could build a

suitable engine to those dimensions. The steam engine lies horizontally, but basically what I planned to do was build this engine in situ, item by item, which is how I suspect the original was assembled.

77

Scale steam engine (non-steaming). This illustration by M White of Medway College of Art was used for general reference by the restoration team. With regard to my intentions to make a scale, but non-steaming, engine and boilers, I was greatly assisted with regard to the dimensions of the high- and low-pressure cylinders by this scaled illustration which I used to make the wooden pattern ready for casting the cylinder block in white metal. I have been unable to trace M White, but would want to fully acknowledge my gratitude, and hope that we may meet one day.

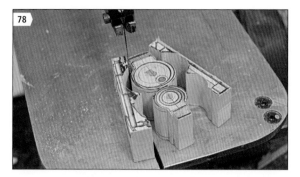

78

Cylinder-head pattern (model), taken from M White's illustration. The timber I am using for the pattern of the cylinder head is jelutong, and the scroll saw (Hegner) makes light work of sawing round the profile. It is worth mentioning that when pattern-making for casting in metal, two vital considerations must be borne in mind; the first is how the pattern is eventually to be released from the shape of a two-part mould, with no 'lock-ins', and, secondly, trying where possible to keep a flat surface where it will be necessary for the casting to be machined. In this particular instance, this applies to boring out the cylinders, which will need to be done with the casting fixed to the bed of the milling machine. Likewise, the split line of the mould will have to align with the lugs at the base of the cylinders, or the pattern would be trapped in the mould and impossible to release.

79

Webs for the crankshaft (model). This was new territory for me: never having had to manufacture a crankshaft before, I approached the issue with some trepidation, but I reasoned that the demands made by a 90-degree crankshaft could be met by using three horizontal steel bars and eight identical lengths of brass strapping, very carefully drilled out with two piercings at their centres. This would give me the all-important parallels of alignment with the three axles/journals involved; once it was silver-soldered together, the unnecessary bar lengths could be cut away, leaving me without any further alignment issues, as far as the main axle shaft would be concerned. The making of this engine does require metal-turning machinery, and it may well be a turn-off for those ship-modellers who do not have the luxury of a screw-cutting lathe and a milling machine, or the space to accommodate them, with all their attachments. Nevertheless, I do clearly remember, before investing in my original second-hand lathe, wondering whether or not ship-modelling deserved this kind of investment. After all, most turned fittings can be bought off the shelf these days, lathes are not ideal for mast-making, as many people assume that they will be, and the haunting question is whether the expense is really justified. Those questions were going through my head over thirty years ago now, but there will be some readers who are seriously contemplating such a purchase in the near future, so for them, I offer the following thoughts. The ability to be

79

able to produce any shape or item accurately in metal puts you in a different place, and because these machines can be made to work with such accuracy, your overall workmanship will be improved. With this kind of machinery, you are forced to measure with much greater frequency, and when you return to the majority of items in model shipbuilding, that same discipline will follow you and make a big all-round improvement. Its a slow and gradual process and you probably won't even notice the difference, but others will.

80

Crankshaft assembly. Aligning the webs of the crankshaft with the cylinder heads, using squared paper. The 90-degree structure helps to steady matters with the necessary brazing technique. Only silver-solder (Easi-flo 2) will give sufficient strength to the joints. I do not believe this could be done with soft-solder, because at any scale, without the plummer-block bearings to support a crankshaft, it is a very vulnerable item, and only a brazing technique gives sufficient and reliable joints to an item like this.

81

Silver brazing the webs of the crankshaft with a propane burner. The unwanted sections of steel rod are then cut away. With brazing, all the items under the burner are brought to at least a dull red colour, and this requires a quick and powerful burst of heat, which is why propane rather than butane gas is used. The process of soldering will seldom fail, providing there is sufficient heat not to burn out the flux before the solder is hot enough to run freely into the joint. On this job, it is important to apply the flux and solder only to the outside edges of the brass strip, because you do not want any residue on the inside edge of the crank webs, next to the crank pins (journals). Hard solder is very difficult to clean off, and the crank pins need a flat-edged face for the big-end bearings of the con rods to revolve against. This is technically not too difficult, because the solder will only follow where the flux has been placed, so that careful application of the flux is

critical to success. You might ask whether if there is no solder applied to the inside of the axle, will that not make a weak joint? The answer is that silver-solder runs into the whole joint, axle included, when the temperature glows hot, the metal expands, allows the solder into the gap, and as it cools, it shrinks onto the joint, imparting its trademark strength. Another tip is one that I learned from a jeweller. When mixing the flux paste for a silver-soldered joint, use methylated spirits rather than water. Meths follows into the joints more easily than water, and is, of course, chemically pure, and cleanliness is part of a successful marriage with all soldered joints. Easi-flo 2 silver-solder has a dedicated flux powder which is always used in conjunction with the solder stick. Finally, hammer the end of the silver-solder stick to flatten it out, and dip it into the flux mixture to purify the tip before starting the process. Flattening a tongue of solder stick will mean that it melts much more easily when applied.

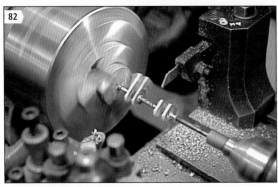

82

Testing the alignment of the crank. A lathe will quickly tell you about the truth of your work when it comes to testing a job like this. I am somewhat relieved to say that I believe the crank is in harmony with itself. I will not really know until it is all connected up, but so far it promises well and I believe that you could make a crank on this principle for a three- or four-cylinder (model) engine: I can see no reason why not. In times past, they were made as forgings and the old ironmasters developed skills in their production which even today are seen as monumental achievements of heavy engineering.

83

Engine bedplate. The cleaned-up crankshaft rests on the engine bed at an angle of 4 degrees, to align with the propshaft. The cylinder head must also do the same. The engine bedplate has to be set in line with the propeller shaft, and there is also a gentle rise of 4 degrees from the stern to take into consideration. The crank and the bearings lie very close to the bedplate, and the cylinder block must align with the crankshaft. With all these critical factors in mind, I am left with having to fit the engine in two halves, into its own environment, in much the same way, I guess, as the original was assembled, measuring item by item as the build progresses. These horizontal engines did have their cylinder blocks bolted down in the wings of the ship's hull, as well as their bottom end bolted down on the bedplate, secured solidly to the floors of the ship. Given the flexible nature of wooden-built craft, there must have been heavy stresses put onto the moving parts of the engine when the vessel was in motion. The iron frames of this ship would have greatly contributed to an overall stiffness of the hull structure, but under extreme circumstances the racking forces on the fixed machinery would have been considerable.

84

Cylinder-head casting. The grey-coloured clay is warmed until liquefied in a bain-marie (a tin in a saucepan of hot water). The first requirement of any mould-making is the creation of a demountable mould wall. Lego bricks make an excellent choice for this, because they are well engineered to be proofed against leakage of the rubber compound, and can be arranged around any shape or object to be cold-cast. Not a lot adheres to the plastic bricks, either. The heat-resistant rubber compound is a Tiranti product (RTV101 Silicone

Rubber) and comes in a 1kg tin along with the droplet hardener. The process of casting begins with making friends with whoever is in charge of the kitchen, as it involves a saucepan and a metal tin, containing the 'clay' or 'chavant' (supplied by Tiranti). The clay needs to be liquefied so that it can be poured into the mould around the pattern of the cylinder head, to the level of the six projecting lugs or ears, which will be the split point of the mould. Initially, pour about one quarter of an inch thickness of the liquefied mixture to cover the bottom of the mould, and allow it to cool off slightly, enough to support the pattern. This is to allow a suitable thickness of rubber at the base of the mould. Then place the pattern and pour in the rest of the molten clay, making it as level as possible with the joint line at the lugs. There will be some levelling off required at this point, done with dental probes and a small, stiff paintbrush, but the tip of a small screwdriver will suffice; anything to make sure that there is a clean joint line around all the detail where the mould will eventually be split in half. The clay is very like Plasticine to work, and after the work at the joint line is completed, it may be smoothed out with the use of white spirits and a small stiff brush to ensure that there is no residue of any kind left.

85

Locating buttons. These are made with a hand-held twist drill, approximately 4mm depth. This will register the top and bottom half of the mould. Note that the split line has been cleaned up with white spirits all the way round where the clay meets the pattern. This is done with a miniature spade-bit screwdriver, or any small chisel blade.

87

First half release. After twelve hours, the walls of the mould are dismantled, and the first half of the pattern released. Note the formation of the locating buttons. The wooden pattern of the cylinder head is now removed, soaked in white spirits, and all traces of clay cleaned off.

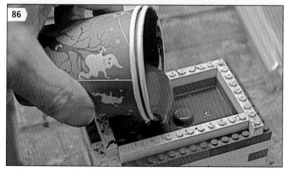

86

First half of mould pouring. Catalysed rubber, well-mixed, being poured into the top half of the mould. It will slowly de-gas on its own, with small bubbles appearing as air makes its way to the surface.

88

Second half. The cleaned-up wooden pattern is re-entered into the mould; a line of extra bricks is added to take the extra height of the second pouring of rubber; a spray of silicone parting agent is used over the pattern and mould, more catalysed rubber mixed, and poured into the mould.

89

Molten metal. The top and bottom half of the mould are bolted together in a homemade 'flask'. An ingate hole is punched through the top of the rubber mould to receive the molten metal from the ladle. The metal is known as K2 (from Tiranti). The metal flows most easily if the mould is first powdered with talcum.

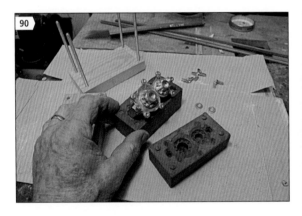

90

Final release of the casting. The flask is dismantled and the conjoined cylinder head released.

91

Boring the cylinder head. The casting has a flat base, resting on the milling table, held in place by faceplate dogs, supported by the female half of the cylinder head's wooden pattern. The bores will be sleeved with brass tubing.

92

Machining the 'jaw'. The slitting saw is mounted in the chuck of the milling machine head; on the right-hand side is the large 'indexing chuck', gripping the brass stock. The TCT saw-blade is machining the jaw of the piston rod's small end bearing. By rotating the indexing chuck through 180 degrees, and carefully adjusting the column height, the cut will self-centre into the bar stock. This enables a very accurate fit.

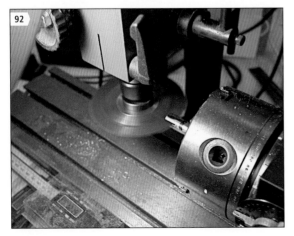

93

Small end bearing. Fitting the piston-rod into the jaw of the small end bearing.

95

Valve eccentrics. These are made off-centre in the independent four-jaw chuck of the lathe.

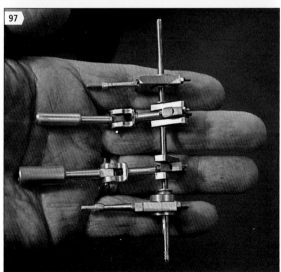

94

Aligning the crankshaft. The engine bed is set on a 4-degree slope matched by the seating which supports the cylinder block. The crankshaft and plummer blocks must also line up with the propeller shaft.

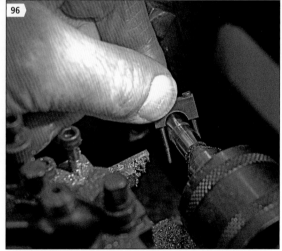

96

Split bearing. The technical name for this item is the 'connecting-rod bottom-end keep'. It runs in the groove of the eccentric bearing.

97

Final crankshaft assembly. In full-size practice, the valve rods open and close the steam inlets and outlets – the 'lead' and the 'lap' of the steam supply

98

Motion. The loosely assembled engine is being run up with the aid of a miniature DC drill. The three plummer blocks have sleeved brass bearings and oiling holes fitted, so that the crankshaft runs smoothly.

99

Boiler manufacture. Model boiler shell made from plastic pipe is matched to the original 1885 plans.

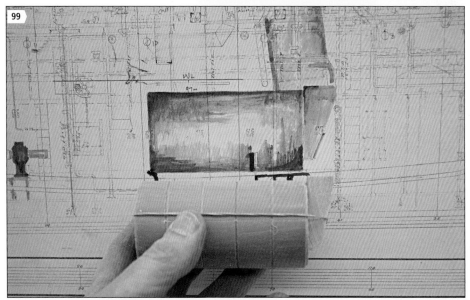

101

Lancashire style. The boiler shell has been detailed with 'in-and-out' plating, mock-riveted in copper shim, using a contact adhesive against the plastic pipe. In full-sized practice, the two boiler flues ran the full 15ft of the shell, and were stoked from the twin fire grates, reaching approximately 5ft into the back end of the boiler.

100

Boiler back-head. A double-sided pattern was created for this; note that the pattern must not contain any detail which would not easily release. This applies to furnace door keeps, etc. The oval-shaped aperture at the base is the sludge hole.

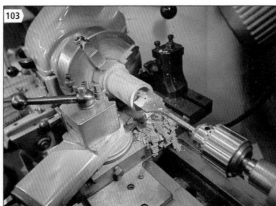

102

Boiler positions. The three boilers are not placed with equidistance, nor is the centre boiler in line with the keel. The true centre is shown with the engineer's square, and this set-up alters the pathway of the conjoined smoke-box uptake.

103

Funnel base section. The funnel base is made from timber (North American cherry), bored out with a very sharp spade bit. This procedure creates a lot of friction and heat, so it needs to be done very gently in several separate entries from the tailstock.

104

Three funnel uptakes. The offset funnel base straddles the three boilers. The overlaid metal cladding is pewter sheet suitably riveted.

105

Gauges. Further details added to the boiler back-heads include steam gauges with siphons (banjos), water-level indicators and valve wheels.

106

Boiler space. This installation is now complete with sight glasses and steam-valve wheels; further pipework is to follow.

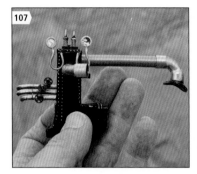

107

Steam chest. This fitting is conjectural, but represents a pressurised chamber where the three steam supply pipes meet, and the flow of steam is controlled. The large aft copper pipe represents the main feed to the (smaller) high-pressure cylinder on the right-hand side of the cylinder block, and the copper elbow fitting leads to the eduction pipe, and thence to the main condenser.

108

Eduction pipe. With the steam chest in position, the large copper eduction pipe crosses over the engine; the purpose of this non-insulated pipe is to cool the exhausted steam from the engine on its way to the main condenser, using the remnant for recirculation into the hot well and reuse in the boilers, as preheated water.

109

Main condenser. This piece of equipment receives the exhausted steam from the engine, passing it over a battery of small pipes containing seawater, reconverting it into still-heated feed water for the boilers.

110

Funnel. The sheet-steel reconstruction of the funnel for the restored ship at Nielsen's Gloucester works (from the Nielsen archive, 5 February 2003).

111

Funnel base (model) positioned on the ship's beams. Note the prominence of the cogged racer arcs (see Chapter 6).

112

Model funnel Shown against the ship's plans. The raising and lowering mechanism is conjectural, as no official details are given for this.

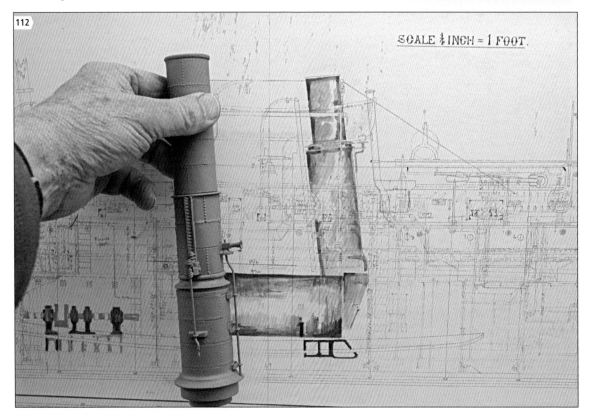

SCALE ¼ INCH = 1 FOOT.

113

Griffiths patent lifting propeller. Scaled image of the propeller placed into the space between the guides. Note the 4-degree angle.

114

Propeller boss. This is turned in the lathe, having previously been centre-bored to take the spigot which will hold the roots of the two blades steady during the silver-soldering process, and maintain the pitch of the blades.

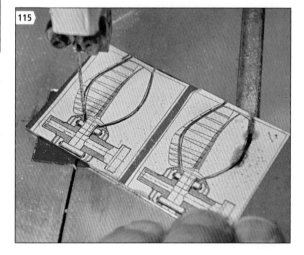

115

Propeller blades. The shape of the blades being bandsawn in brass, using a lubricant to cool the blade. The full-sized design of the blade with clipped ends significantly reduced the problems of cavitation and vibration caused by the earlier Robert Griffiths' screw. This later version was patented and first used to power HMS *Warrior* in 1860, and is yet another historical connection between these two preserved ships. That fitted to *Warrior* was the largest ever made, weighing an estimated 26 tons with a diameter of 24ft 6in, cast from bronze. *Gannet's* propeller is approximately half that size at 13ft 1in – the weight is unknown.

116

Silver-soldering the blades. The second blade receiving a concentrated blast of heat from the propane torch. The trick with all soldering is to apply enough heat quickly, before the solder flux burns out and corrupts the joint.

117

The banjo. The raising frame for the propeller is known as the banjo. In this picture, the propeller shaft bearing (the brass tube) is soft-soldered to the edge of the brass sheet, using copper wire tourniquets to hold it in place and on centre during the soldering process.

118

Parting off the frame. The bearing tube is largely cut away, leaving only the small sections which will eventually lower into the bearing cups.

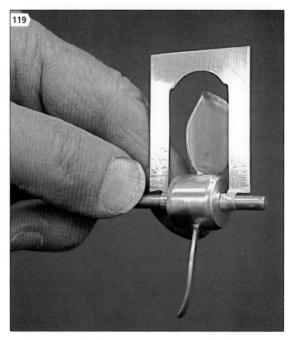

119

Raising frame assembly. The stub shaft connects to the propeller shaft using a 'cheese coupling'. (In the photo this is not yet made.) In full-sized practice, the engine was stopped at top dead-centre, and the cheese-shaped wedge on the stub shaft could then engage with the slot in the main propeller shaft. The advantage of this system was that it did not require a diver.

5: Decks and Decking

120

Poop deck sponson. This extra sweep to the poop deck created a platform for the 5in central pivot gun, allowing a wide arc of fire without the interruption from the shrouds of the mizzenmast. The aluminium globe is a full-sized door stop.

121

Restoration HMS *Gannet*'s **sponson.** The 5in Armstrong CP gun is original.

121

Waterway. Creating the long lengths of moulding required for the model waterway, surrounding the weather deck of the ship, requires setting up a table saw in an unusual way. Instead of the fence running parallel with the saw-blade, a wooden fence/guide is set first to an angle of 80 degrees, with the tip of the saw-blade being heightened incrementally at the end of each pass, as the moulding strip is machined over it. This is one of the advantages of a table saw fitted with 'rise and fall'. This offset fence/guide allows the circular saw-blade to cut a wider saw-kerf with a nicely rounded contour to it. An even wider central cut can then be made by moving the wooden fence/guide to 73 degrees. Finally, the moulding is sawn in half to give the particular profile of the waterway. See the picture of the racer arcs in Chapter 6 following for the full effect of the blackened watercourse running the full length of the deck.

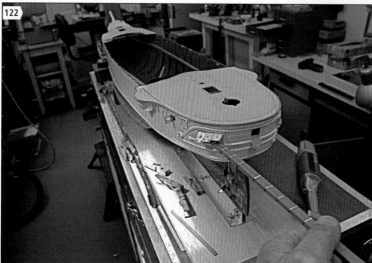

122

Deck stringers. These are long lengths of timber, carefully machined with slots as matching pairs for both the weather-deck and lower-deck beams. The slot housings are all numbered according to the plan, which becomes essential as the deck fittings, etc, are added. The stringers are so long that it is impossible to load them without 'posting' them through the quarterdeck gun ports.

123

Pattern for the deck beams. Stress-relieving saw-cuts allow a strip of mahogany to be pushed into a curve, whilst the timber is still laid flat. This strip is then glued to a backing of thin plywood. The curvature of the backing strip is planed off to the profile of the bent strip at the top, but left horizontal at the bottom. This enables it to be used in conjunction with an engineer's square, against a marked-up sheet of ply from which the beams will be cut. It is a fact that model ships' decks need a slightly increased camber, otherwise they appear flat and uninteresting – don't ask me why!

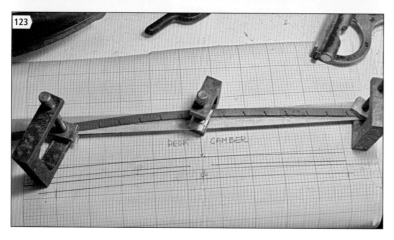

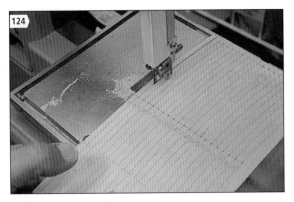

124

Deck beams. These were sawn from birch 3-ply, overlaid with a timber strip at the top, and reinforced with a bulb section beneath.

125

Decking. This was made in sheet form, by setting the table saw over to an angle of 45 degrees, and using the tip of the saw-blade to score through one layer of ply. The plank width is 3mm.

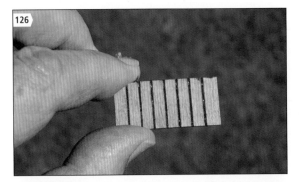

126

Planking. Close-up of the effect of saw-cuts and seams in the deck structure. Made this way, decks never appear 'flat' from any angle, not should model decks in general be made too shiny. One coat of varnish is normally sufficient.

127

Caulking. The seams of the restored decking are tackled with mallets and 'small stuff' (oakum) in this photograph from the Nielsen archive taken on 10 July 2003. The seams are then paid with hot pitch in the traditional fashion to defend the oakum from the wet, allowing for the swell and shrinkage of the decking in all weathers.

128

Decking throughout the model is attached like a veneer to sub-decks, with the curvature held by deck beams. This requires clip-clamping around all the edges, first working from the centre line with deep-throated clamps. This avoids any pockets of air being trapped between the layers.

129

Comb-jointing. Where deck joints in planking have to be made, the castellated line of a comb joint can almost completely hide the cut. This is a useful technique for disguising the saw-cuts of removable hatches, etc, on any model ship.

130

Cant-edging in mahogany. This has to be fitted in the traditional way, regardless of cost, but makes a handsome feature.

131

Poop deck on HMS *Gannet*, ten years after the restoration; note the actual colour of a ship's deck – turning almost silver-grey.

132

Canvas covers over the hammock netting; in miniature, this is dealt with by ironing on a self-adhesive shrink-wrap material, as used by modellers skinning the wings of aircraft; it is being applied to strips of fine-scale aluminium mesh. It does not adhere to the iron's soleplate if kept on a low heat.

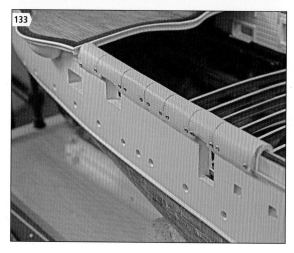

133

Hammock netting. The mesh is first wrapped over a thick, round dowel former, before attaching it to the hoops; the 2mm eyelets have to be applied before attaching the cover to the hoops.

6: Firepower

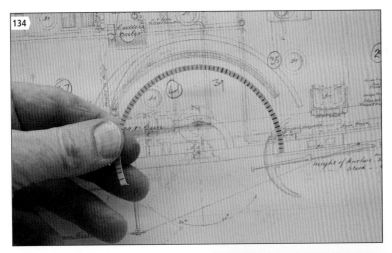

134

Gun-aiming rack. This semi-circular track, which is deck-mounted, is for the two forward 64pdr muzzle-loaders only. The old-fashioned description from Captain Garbett's *Naval Gunnery* (1897) is 'a racer arc, cogged for the purpose'. The training shaft of the gun carriage engaged it with a toothed wheel worked by means of pinions and winch handles at the rear extremity of the sliding carriage.

135

Racer arcs. Jig for making the demi-lune shape of the racer arcs needed for the gun carriages. The jig is dependent on the adjustable pivot pin which is taped into a slot on an independent false table of plywood. The false table is held in place by the protruding square section of timber seen at the head of the picture, captured in the bandsaw's mitre-fence guide. The saw-cut is first made with the pin set further from the blade; it can then be moved inwards 2mm for the second cut. All the half-round timber supports were fashioned like this.

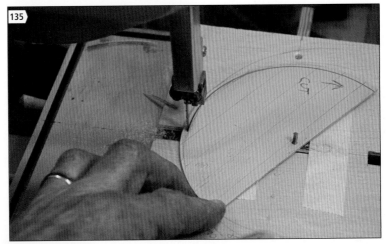

136

The rack. Two half-round shapes were first cut on the jig as described above, and bolted together, with a large-size dowel glued to the centre (a bolt will not do). The outer edges of both semicircles are then flooded with superglue in order not to lose any sawn detail on their edges. A slitting saw is then tightened into the milling-machine chuck. On the right-hand side is mounted the large indexing chuck, which is attached to an indexer, controlled by a dividing plate; this gives an ordered division of any circle. With the saw-blade running, the milling machine table is wound in and out, allowing the circular saw-blade to score through one layer of ply; similar cuts are also made on the reverse side of the semicircle.

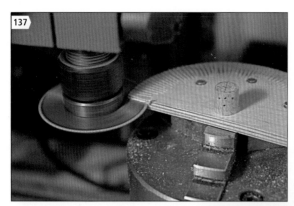

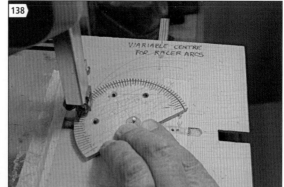

137

Slitting saw. The indexing chuck is now mounted horizontally on the milling machine table, lined up and rotated against the cut of the circular saw-blade. This is done in several passes, to avoid too much heat building up. A small detail – if you ever invest in a milling machine, make sure the motor can run in both directions.

138

Parting off. The central wooden dowel is trimmed flush on both sides and centred in the lathe to accommodate the pivot pin. The parting-off process follows, producing a convincing-looking toothed rack. This may seem like a lot of trouble, but it is an important historical feature which remains highly visible.

139

Bird's eye view. The six racer arcs with their outer and inner tracks. The metal rails in brass are 1/16in tubing, first softened with heat, and then wrapped round a former, followed by flattening with light taps of a hammer. Note also the waterways surrounding the deck margins (in black) and scuppers fitted into the margin planks, where in full scale water would lie if not drained away. (Disregard the two 68pdr guns in the forward gun ports – they belong to another model.)

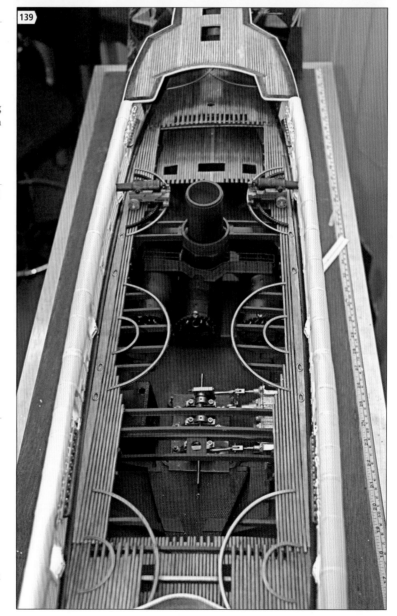

140

The infamous Armstrong 110lb breech-loader, 1860. Author's model of the gun which changed everything for the Royal Navy. The 110pdr breech-loading gun proved to be so dangerous that it was withdrawn three years after its introduction. This was the gun used as a bow- and stern-chaser aboard HMS *Warrior* (1860) when she was first launched. Note the notorious vent piece held with the surgical tweezers, which caused all the trouble. Despite much improved accuracy, although not penetration, the weapon had to be withdrawn three years after its introduction, leaving the Royal Navy with the embarrassment of a brand-new gun which did not work, and a technological vacuum which had no instant solution. When the new breech-loading gun was first used in anger, at the battle of Kagoshima Bay in August 1863 (a British 'intervention' in Japan), in the bombardment that followed, it was reported that, according to Antony Preston, 'so many Armstrong guns burst (an aggregate of twenty-eight accidents to twenty-one guns in 365 rounds) that the Navy went back to muzzle loaders for fifteen years. At the height of the action, HMS *Euryalus*'s forward 7-inch gun blew out its breech-block and concussed the whole crew.'

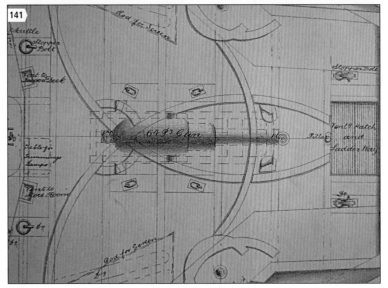

141

Return to muzzle-loading. Plan view of the 64pdr bow-chaser gun HMS *Gannet* (1885 refit) sited under the fo'c'sle deck shown in position on the fo'c'sle deck racer arcs. This is the reason why, twenty-five years later, when the plans of the refitted *Gannet* were drawn up in 1885, old fashioned muzzle-loaders are clearly shown sited in their separate locations: the three 64pdrs mounted forward – two broadside and one under the fo'c'sle deck – and the two 90cwt guns (the heaviest) stowed amidships. The much more modern two 5in, 30cwt, central-pivot Vavasseur RBL Armstrong guns were placed on the poop-deck sponsons as stern-chasers, with their latest oil-filled recoil pistons giving them a modern distinction not possessed by the other main armament on the gun deck. These were guns fired in anger against the Egyptian Mahdist rebels, at the battle of Port Suakin on 17 September 1888 (see Chapter 1).

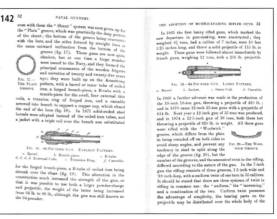

142

Naval Gunnery. Captain Garbett's book explains the origins of the 64pdr gun and how it comes to be fitted to a gun vessel.

143

Original 64pdr gun barrel mounted on a restored metal carriage, sited under the fo'c'sle deck at Chatham Historic Dockyard, aboard HMS *Gannet*, as it would have appeared in 1885. Note the all-metal construction of the gun carriage and the bronze breeching-rope fitment, near the front trucks. This later version of the 64pdr has a longer parallel jacket over the firing chamber including the trunnion ring, and a parallel shoulder leading aft towards the cascabel. Both guns were rifled on the principle of the Woolwich groove pattern, using studs in the projected shells, to impart an accuracy of spin. My source is Garbett's 1897 book on naval gunnery. He says, referring to this transitional period of the 64pdrs: 'These guns are now quite obsolete, but at one time, a large number were issued to the Navy, and they formed the principal armaments of the wooden frigates and corvettes of twenty and twenty five years ago [ie 1872–87].'

144

Scale drawings of heavy ordnance transcribed onto the drawing board for pattern-making. With this information confirmed, it is time to fetch out the drawing board, and draft the vital statistics of the heavy armament. By aligning the gun barrels on the drawing board, it is possible to see the different shapes and sizes of the three types of heavy guns in relation to one another. Drawing is also a vital discipline in thinking out clearly what it is you have got to do to produce the physical item in miniature. This may well be a personal excuse for not getting too involved with computer-aided drawing programs, but I still like the freedom of the T-square, whose simplicity has much to commend it; I regard it as a vital and inexpensive tool for scratch-builders. How can you make anything accurately from scratch, without a drawn plan to follow?

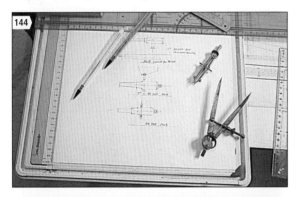

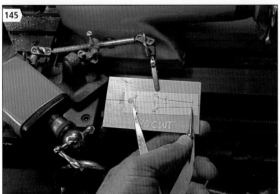

145

90cwt gun. The miniature gun barrel image pasted onto a flat board, assisted by a helping hand. The measuring instrument is known as an 'odd-leg' or 'Jenny' calliper.

160

90cwt gun barrel being machined with measurements from the pattern on the lathe.

147

Casting pattern for the 5in gun barrel. Once again, RTV rubber is mixed for the first half of the mould. The miniature barrel is resting on a bed of dental plaster into which it has been pushed to the halfway point, when the plaster was curing off.

148

Pouring preparations. Powdering the two halves of the rubber mould for the 5in gun barrel; other moulds have been made for the central pivot gun including the pivot base, the gun recoil slides and pistons

149

Gravity pouring into the ingate of the two-part rubber mould. The ingate is an enlarged hole reamed out with a scalpel to ease the pouring; note that the mould is reinforced with strips of ply and clamps, with the body of it held in the jaws of a vice.

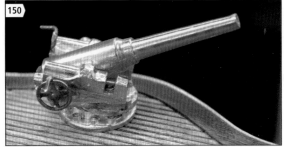

150

The bare mouldings of the 5in CP gun mounted on the sponson. The superior manoeuvrability of this gun over earlier ordnance is shown to advantage. The large wheel on the right is for direction (training), the smaller one for barrel elevation.

151

Gun carriages and other heavy ordnance plus details: 64pdr gun is held in place by the scriber; the 90cwt gun is placed below; the gun elevation mechanisms, etc, are fitted to the carriages; with Armstrong guns these are known as RCDs (Royal Carriage Dept).

152

The 5in Armstrong pivot gun is original and fitted on the starboard sponson of HMS *Gannet*. Note the detail of the breech mechanism and the handsome manganese bronze recoil pistons and barrel elevation wheel.

152

153

Nordenfelt machine gun. This hopper-fed gun could allegedly fire 480 rounds a minute.

154

154

Model of the Nordenfelt volley gun mounted above the embrasure on the fo'c'sle deck. This was the four-barrelled Nordenfelt machine gun, originally of Swedish design, and produced in many different versions for all sorts of combat situations. It was patented in 1873. In operation, just at the rear of the breech, was the all-important lever on the right-hand side of the gun which had three positions: when it was pulled back, it extracted the spent cartridges; when pushed forward, it loaded fresh cartridges from the hopper; when pushed further forward, it fired all four of the barrels one after the other in quick succession. It was known as a volley gun, firing bullets in bursts. My immediate reaction to modelling this gun was to get the training gear and elevation wheels right. They are more prominent features than the gun itself, which is essentially four barrels bolted together on a tray-like structure, with a trigger mechanism giving a spray of four steel bullets when the handle is pushed forwards. The trigger handle can be seen in the illustration just above the training wheel. The gun is set in a double yoke to allow for its removal; the jaw of the inner yoke provides a swivel point for elevation. Elevation and depression are controlled by a separate wheel on the port side of the gun (not visible); the outer yoke attaches to the worm gear for aiming and training

the gun, but the Nordenfelt gun could be released from the pivot stand and used from other stations on the gun deck, or transported onto a shore-based carriage for raiding parties or other territorial emergencies. Its portability gave it great practical use, capable of firing an astonishing 480 rounds per minute, each barrel loosing off 120 rounds. This put it on a par with Dr Gatling's ten-barrelled revolving machine gun, rated at 500 rounds per minute, but liable to jam, and requiring experienced gunners to operate it. An interesting detail: I see from the original illustration that the barrels were hexagonal on their outer profile, rather than round. This would have made the machining process of rifling them in the gun factory much easier, because a hexagonal shape locates with accuracy into a three-jaw lathe chuck, and would prevent any slippage when being rifle-bored; it would also give a precise fit onto the gun-mounting rack when the barrels were bolted together, and a simpler job for running repairs, of which there must have been many. The strips of brass used for the framework for the gun are made from squashed brass 2mm tube. Tube has many forgiving qualities, particularly when it has been heated and quenched, and fabricating the framework for this gun cradle is going to require twists and turns which straightforward flat section of brass cannot easily handle, but you can do it with annealed tubing which has a greater tolerance to being manipulated. The outer yoke of the mechanism is given squared corners, hammered around a section of steel bar. This will give the effect of an engineered piece of work, and uniformity. The originals were, of course, castings, not fabrications.

155

The model barrels are wired together with very fine copper wire and the small 'pallets' of soft solder off the coil are flattened with a hammer, and snipped off into 2mm squares. These are placed on top of the wax flux paste (Everflux TM) and when sweated with an open flame will cause the solder pallets to run into all the crevices, joining the barrels together.

157

Nordenfelt gun mounted on the fo'c'sle deck at Chatham Historic Dockyard, 2013.

156

Bevel gearing. I puzzled for quite a while as to how I could convincingly produce the bevel gearing for the training of the gun. The final solution was to mount the dividing head on the milling machine and just 'kiss' the outer face of the cogwheel with the finest centre drill I possess. I wish that I could have made the angle more acute, but mounting the indexing device on a small table limited my ability to do this. Always buy a milling machine with the largest table you can afford; milling machines have this annoying habit of not being able to position accessories where you most want them to be. I am aware that there are other configurations which are available to me, but I think long and hard before altering the position of the milling machine head out of the vertical. It took some courage to take the spray cans to remove all that triumphant metal work, and kill off most of the detail. Nevertheless, the sprayed finish does achieve the promised look of a real gun, rather than a model of a gun, and it is literally a case of biting the bullet in the cause of realism. At this period of history, warships were still highly polished, but it has to be remembered that any glinting object at sea gives away the position of a vessel and takes away any element of surprise as far as the enemy lookout is concerned.

158

Magazine. Close-up of the aft starboard magazine (model). In common with a great many warships, the magazine of *Gannet* is sited below the waterline in the ship's hold, immediately aft the engine room, but separated and insulated by a watertight bulkhead, well away from sources of ignition. The careful placing of the ship's magazine here is not only a safety feature, but also out of practical necessity. Shell and solid shot are, in terms of deadweight, of a similar order to the ship's chain lockers and the stowage of fresh water in six tanks placed forward, weighing a total 2,970 gallons, not including separate compartments for sand and lime to make cement. For the stability of the ship's hull, these items need to counterbalance one another and keep the metacentric level of the vessel as low as possible in the water. Not easy when you consider the top weight of coal stored all around the engine and boiler rooms, plus the relatively shallow draught of the hull. In full scale, the shells carried on board to supply the guns were carefully laid out and arranged in wooden boxes with metal linings, compartmentalised into different sizes according to the calibre and weight of the shells. The original word *makazin* is Arabic for a 'portable storehouse or repository for articles of value'. All Armstrong shells by this period were cone-headed and coated on the exterior with a thin layer of lead; when the gun was fired, the rifling of the gun barrel cut a thread in the lead casing, thus imparting a spinning motion to the shell, which, in turn, gave the projectile greatly increased accuracy from the old days of round shot. There were many different types of shell: solid shot; case shot, which would burst with sizeable iron balls; common shell, carrying a powder charge fitted with a fuze, and for a full burst, shrapnel filled with hundreds of pellets the size of a musket ball. With safety in mind, for the heavy ordnance Armstrong time fuses were not screwed into

the shell until just before firing. The starboard magazine in the model shows the heavier shells of the 90cwt guns and the 64pdrs. Added to this list are the Nordenfelt hopper magazines, cases of gunpowder propellant carefully stowed in cartridges, and ammunition for marines' usage. Small arms on board included pistols and Martini–Henry rifles. All of these charges are listed on the plan view of the hold and demonstrate that these ships were not pussycats if confronted by any opposition, although they were never designed to resist out-and-out warfare, only to be able to hold their station with dignity.

159

Sawn to size: machining brass bar to size. The cone has already been ground on the linisher before cropping off. If model-sized brass bar or tube is not secured into a sized groove when it is being cut in a bandsaw, when not held captive it will either fly up as the cut is finished, or worse still, disappear altogether. Always wrap brass bar or brass tube with masking tape before cutting it; for reasons not clear to me, it makes for a much smoother cut with no snatching.

160

Installation of both aft magazines into the model hull, showing their proximity to the engine bulkhead (not modelled) and the tunnel shaft. In full scale, although the magazine is sited below the waterline, it must have been a constant cause of concern from so many sources of possible ignition.

7: Ground and Steering Gear

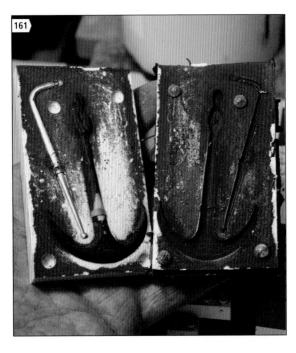

162

161

Bower anchor: pattern and mould for the bower and waist anchors. Continuing with the theme of metal casting, the miniature anchors are the last of the heavy items to be produced. They are standard Admiralty pattern with removable stocks, which key into the shanks, and this is how the bower anchors are displayed on the fo'c'sle deck of the prototype. The restorers have only two on display, but the plans show waist anchors fitted to the outside walls of the ship, just above the forward main deck mooring bollards, so four have been cast for the model. The anchors are produced in exactly the same way as the heavy ordnance gun barrels, starting with a dental plaster mould, followed by the upper and lower rubber mould, using a double entry ingate for both the anchor and the stock. Generally speaking, it is a mistake to try and make two mouldings in one flask, and I only just got away with this. It is much better to do them individually. Note also how near the fluke of the anchor is positioned in the rubber pattern – perilously close to the edge. This is bad practice. To overcome these hazards, I had to cut an over-large ingate at the shank end to force the molten metal into the mould, and then create the ends of the stocks from solid metal. Fortunately, this is not difficult to do because the metal is free-cutting in a bandsaw, but I saved no time at all by not doing them as separate items.

Keyway cut for the anchor stock in the casting. The pathway for the miniature file was first cut with a piercing blade. Diamond-coated files need to be kept very clean with a brass wire brush. I also use a fluid which keeps saw-blades free of resin build-up, and it seems to work on diamond-coated files as well – not brilliant in this usage, but it helps – but it is very effective for saw-blades. The key fits snugly into the anchor stem; note that there has to be undercut beneath the keyhole, to allow for the right angle on the stock to be unshipped into the stowed position. The palms or flukes of the anchors are set into the 'arms' of the crown, and the upward sweep of the crown is known as the trend. The drilled hole through the iron collar at the base of the shank is in preparation for the fish shackle, made from copper wire. In full scale, this ring is used for raising up the bottom weight of the anchor when being hoisted to the cathead, and secured for stowage. It is, roughly speaking, set at the point of balance. The main anchor ring at the shank head is made from copper piping, suitably softened with heat. It is taken to orange on the heat scale, which makes it very malleable, then wrapped round a sized section of wooden dowel. It is then snipped off and flattened with the Maun pliers, and is ready to be hammered on the ends, giving the pipe the appearance of a forged metal ring. All that now remains is to 'bead the ends' of the removable stock, fitting the extremes with what are technically known as the nuts, finishing with the addition of the half-hoop of the fish shackle at the bottom of the anchor's shank.

163

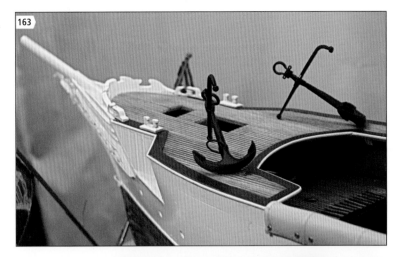

163

Completed pair of anchors resting on the fo'c'sle deck; note the anchor ring at the headstock and the fish-shackle, near the point of balance at the opposite end. I treated all the finished castings in the same way: that is to say, two undercoats of red oxide, finished with no more than a whiff of satin black spray, which has a slight sheen to it. This gives a hint of rust – corrosion just lying in wait to take over the paintwork – and it also gives cohesion to all the detail. Nothing in this life is ever just one colour; it all depends on how light is falling on an object, and it is as well with model ships to keep a limited palette amongst all the confusion of what is to follow. The weight of these anchors is given on the 1885 plan as 31cwt, but there is a slight difference in weight between the best bower anchor starboard and its partner on the port side.

164

164

Delivery of the first anchor for the restoration (from the Nielsen Archive, 13 August 2003).

165

165

Studded link chain (model) lowered into a weak solution of ferric chloride acid. (Safety note: *Always Add the Acid* to the water.) This will allow it to grow its own verdigris on brass or copper. Lay it out on a piece of kitchen roll and watch it happen.

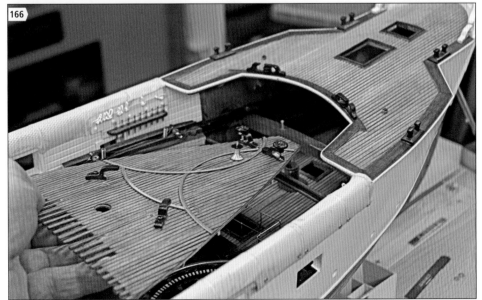

166

166

Cable deck model section slides under the fo'c'sle for the last time; it will be held captive by the foremast. Note the racer arcs which allow the bow-chaser gun to be brought on station; also the chain stoppers, which control the anchor cables.

167

167

Ship's fore-quarters. This uninterrupted view of the model's three forward-facing deck levels shows the lead of the anchor cables into the lockers below, and the water tanks beyond. Sail lockers lie beyond them, but have not been modelled. Also note that on the main deck for'ard are the seamen's 'heads' on the port side behind the white screen, and opposite those of the petty officers with individual doors. Officers' heads were sited under the canopy of the poop deck on the port side. Basically speaking, the lower deck housed the needs of the crew, and their quarters were fairly dark, served only by the natural light of the deeply sunken portholes.

168

Anchor cables (restoration). Manhandling the studded link chain of the bower anchors on HMS *Gannet* alongside the foremast in a Nielsen photograph from 6 June 2007.

ADMIRALTY SPECIFICATIONS

No. 3
The capstan, and other appliances and gear of every description necessary for the working, stowing and securing the anchors and cables, including spare fittings, are also to be provided and completely fitted by the Contractor; the anchors and cables alone being excepted, and found by the Government, but fitted by the Contractor.

No. 97
The Capstan and fittings: to be Brown and Hadfield's patent wrought iron, fitted with wrought iron whelps if required, in position as shown on the plans fitted complete with cable holders. A descriptive sketch is to be provided by the Contractor from which no deviation will be allowed without the permission of the Overseer.

169

The capstan. The restoration Brown and Hadfield's capstan in a Nielsen archive photograph from 11 September 2003. Note the lower whelps below the pawl rim, which engage the studded link chain. The capstan for the model came as an afterthought; the original idea for this quarter of the model ship was to have a clear sightline to the detail of the lower decks forward, the condenser room, the cable lockers and water storage tanks below. The fitting of the solid deck beam also plays an additional role in having a rank of miniature lights beneath it; this illuminates an otherwise dark quarter of the ship and the front ends of the boilers. Once the decision had been made to use a beam, there seemed to be no logic in omitting the handsome detail of the capstan. Since time immemorial, the capstan has literally played a central part of a sailing ship's deck fittings, and on occasions came complete with a fiddler or drummer to keep up the rhythm of the long and arduous tasks which manning the capstan required. This photograph shows the seating of the capstan barrel into the pawl rim; the pawls are the metal

fingers which stop the barrel from running out of control. Note also the chain whelps sited underneath the white rim, which engage with the chain links.

170

Drumhead (model) under construction. You do not need an indexer to make a model capstan, but it helps, in both horizontal and vertical mode. The square pigeonholes are the locations for the capstan bars and these are held in position with removable pins. The protruding vertical bars which provide grip on the barrel are known as the whelps.

171

Chain locker hawse (model). Finished model capstan; note the colour of the chain after acid treatment.

172

Support beam (model) for the propeller well. In terms of modelling, in order to add the look of weight to any fitting like a girder or beam, it is necessary to 'wire' the edge. This will give it the appearance of a casting, which is important if an item has to represent strength on a small scale. The way this can be done is to heat up a length of 1mm pure copper wire to cherry red with the flame of a torch. This will make it extremely malleable and easy to manipulate. Then place the wire down on a flat metal file, or a surface which will stop it moving about. With a separate file, make a 'flat' on the surface of the wire to give it a greater area for adhesion. You do not need to overdo this, just a whisk or two will suffice. Start by spotting the wire with cyano to hold the wire strip in place; when it adheres you will easily be able to shape the wire around the profile with a pair of fine-nosed pliers and flood it with superglue. Copper and hardwood work very well together, and although this looks like a tricky thing to do, it isn't, and the final look of the item is well worth the trouble.

173

The haul of the lifting propeller was by manpower; 'handraulic' is the official term – by human effort alone. The arched metal beam which takes the burden of the haul for the propeller is depicted on the ship's plan, with a sheave and a stop included, but the only clue as to how this heavy Griffith's propeller was raised and lowered is given in Admiralty specification no. 136, which simply says 'Sheer legs, eyebolts etc., for lifting propeller.' It might be assumed, at this late date of 1885, that raising an item as heavy as this propeller on a regular basis would require auxiliary steam power, or gearing via a winch; but this is to underestimate the need, in the mind of the Royal Navy, to keep a late nineteenth-century sailing ship crew busy at all times. On the orders of 'Down funnel, up screw', all hands would be called upon to 'haul up the ruddy old twiddler', using pennants and purchases which led forward and were hauled manually to the opposite sides of the poop deck. The two sheer legs were stepped into the side walls of the propeller well, and at the sheer head itself, the purchases of each pennant passed over a roller sheave, then down to the banjo frame, and up again, to be made fast at the apex of sheer head; this procedure would be carried out with the support given by the chain guys fore and aft. The propeller could then be manually hoisted up on the double sheave attached to the banjo frame and secured to eyebolts on the deck. I do not know this for certain, but the overhead beam may well have simplified this evolution, by being a permanent fixture; adding sheerlegs would certainly have had the effect of relieving the burden, especially with the addition of extra tackle on the hauls, but it would be possible do all this without the use of sheerlegs. The beam may also have played a secondary role in safely supporting the propeller when shipped over a long period of time; again, this suggestion is only surmise on my part. In full scale, the guides in which the propeller frame slides up and down had a ratchet and pawl system fitted, to prevent the accidental dropping of a lifting screw, which would cause enormous damage both to the ship's bearings and the stern frame. (When SS *Discovery* was being built in Dundee in 1900, this accident did occur, and it was thought it might be the source of the famous 'Dundee leak' from which this vessel suffered as a threatening menace on the long voyage to Antarctica; food and provisions were drastically affected on the outward journey to New Zealand because of this persistent leak.)

174

Helm wheel. The astonishing level of craftsmanship shown by the detail of this Nielsen picture of the replica double-handed helm wheel, taken on 23 February 2006, demonstrates exactly how much care was taken by Nielsen's workforce throughout the restoration of HMS *Gannet*.

175

The model helm wheel(s) were milled out on a computer-controlled machine, programmed to produce two twelve-spoke wheels. They then needed to be fettled to lighten the look of the spokes and handles. I do not have, or even want, a CNC machine, but I admire what they can produce.

176

Wheel dial support pillars have an integrated helm indicator dial to show the rudder position – three and a half turns port or starboard is the limit of travel.

177

Ladders (model construction). The spacer method of ladder production starts with inserting a small finger of brass shim as seen on the left-hand side of the bandsaw blade. With this device, an equidistant cut can be made to a stopped depth. The first cut is made freehand so that it can locate into the brass finger; after that the process is simple. The backing guide on the bandsaw table is angled according to the requirement for the treads; this will vary according to how tight the angle of the ladder is placed on the deck. Model ladder uprights are always made in matching pairs with the strips of timber taped together in this case. Likewise, rung ladder uprights are drilled through with two strips taped together and locked into a sawn groove, so that they cannot move as the process is taking place.

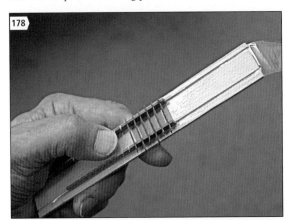

178

Miniature ladder assembly jig. The backing board is first taped over with shiny tape and two grooves then ripsawn into the backing board. This will prevent any glue spots adhering to the jig. All components for the ladder need to be varnished first, before any glue is applied, or the glue in the joints will show. Note that the ladder steps are made of thinner timber than the uprights.

179

Nine-step ladder, leading from the weather deck to the poop; note the top step must align with the deck edge.

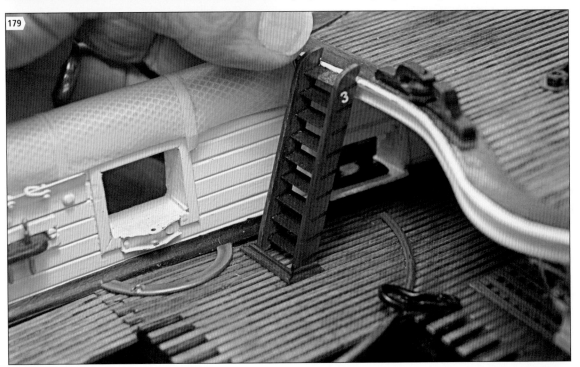

180

Restoration ladder, in a Nielsen photograph of 6 June 2007. The panelled doors of the officers' heads are seen under the canopy, beyond the ladder.

181

Ladders to all deck levels (model). Fo'c'sle to weather deck; cable deck to lower deck and 'metal' rung ladders to the hold.

182

Name-board. Surviving name-board just visible below the
quarter-gallery window in this Nielsen picture from 18 July
2002. This would have been changed at least four times in
the ship's long life. Name-board is really a misnomer, because
in full scale the letters which form the name of *Gannet* are
separately placed on the stern, and not on a plate at all. This
presents a difficulty, as I want them to protrude and be made
of brass, so the alternative strategy for the model has been to
acid-etch them as a single item on a brass plate. Ferric
chloride is the acid in use here. It is normally used for the
creation of experimental PCB circuit boards, and sold
through the local Radio Shack retail outlets either in liquid
or dry form; it is used to eat away the unwanted connections
in copper circuit boards, but it also works well with brass
lettering. It is not a vicious acid, but it needs to be treated
with respect. Eye and hand protection is strongly emphasised
and observe the three 'A's – *Always Add the Acid* to water; the
receptacles must be made of plasticised material, using plastic
tweezers to place the articles in and out of soak. These items
are often sold as a kit for electronic work.

182

183

Letter transfers. Preparations for the model name-board
using Letraset transfer sheet. Preparation work to the brass
plate includes a wire-wool polish to give a clean surface to
the transfer letters, but note, it is *not* a good idea to trim off
the ends of the brass strip until the lettering has been
centred. Do not forget to screen off the back of the plate and
the edges, with gloss paint or with plastic insulation tape, to
prevent acid attack where it is not wanted.

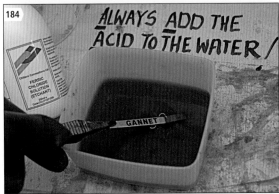

184

183

184

Acid etching. Soaking the letters in ferric chloride solution
for approximately five hours: the plastic bath contains a
50:50 water/acid mix. Etching as a technique is ages old, in
terms of using acid to bite away any exposed metal which has
been left unscreened. Letraset transfers, which form the
screen for the letters, are produced in this country primarily
for labelling materials and items in situations where a printer
cannot be used. The letter transfers themselves are made of a
material which will resist the acid for about five hours, before
the adherence with the brass plate becomes corrupted. If a
deep etch is required, it is possible then to remove the brass
plate from the bath, clean it up, and reapply a fresh set of
lettering over the ones whose adherence has started to break
up, and put the plaque back for a further soak, although this
is not usually necessary. The soaking mixture should be at
about 50 per cent water and 50 per cent acid, always
remembering to put the *WATER into the bath FIRST*. On
removal, rinse away the brass plaque and wire-wool the
result, which should have good depth to it after five hours or
so, giving a distinctly raised level of lettering. A background
paint can then be applied either by spray or brush, which,
when it is truly dry, can be cut back with a very fine grade of
wet and dry paper and then polished brightly on the raised
part of the lettering.

185

Raised brass letters on the name-board. Because of the rake of the stern, without the background colour it is almost impossible to read the name-plate, possibly the reason for the block letters of the original, which rely on natural shadow for recognition, as much as the gilding. What can possibly go wrong? Sometimes the lettering can float off, or parts of it can de-laminate early in the process, particularly if the lettering has serifs which are very fine. The block letters behave well because they have the best grip on the surface area on the brass. I was originally told that gentle heat activated the acid and gentle agitation helped the action. My experience with lettering is just to leave it all alone and let it do its work.

186

Seats of ease: Nielsen photograph of the restoration from 18 September 2003. By the 1870s the heads and urinals on this type of vessel had been moved inboard, and properly

plumbed-in baths for the engineers and stokers fitted. On the model, the housings for the heads and urinals have been constructed according to the plan of the main deck, just below the hooded wings of the fo'c'sle deck. On the starboard side, the first door is the designation of the warrant officers' WCs, the second is the province of the chief petty officers. On the port side is located the seamen's WCs, urinals and more seats of ease; this has only a screen as an entrance and marked the difference of rank between the crew members and the higher ranks of non-commissioned warrant officers. Draughty without a door, but it was important to keep these areas with plenty of fresh air to counteract the bad odours which naturally arose from their constant usage. Commissioned officers' WCs were sited on the port side under the quarterdeck. The Royal Navy in the nineteenth century was not a classless society, and these personal matters of rank and seniority were taken very seriously. Interestingly, it remains the case today, despite the liberated times in which we now live, that this differentiation of personal importance still exists.

8: Coal and Electricity

187

Coal. The ever-expanding steam-powered Royal Navy required a whole network of coaling stations to sustain it. Their availability, security and constant ability to provide fresh supplies were vital for refuelling these vessels; without coaling stations stretching across the face of the globe from Halifax to Hong Kong, on all the major commercial shipping routes, these vessels would have been powerless to fight an engagement, and with the introduction of electricity in the case of major battleships, the steam-powered dynamo lighting circuits would also have been inoperable. The photograph shows coal drifts set in pure resin on the model – miniature coal is available loose as a model railway accessory from Busch (Khole HO 7073). Caution: do not try machining this miniature coal. The reason it looks so real and has weight to it, is the fact that it is natural grit (covered with plastic). If you try cutting it into shape, it will very quickly blunt the teeth on a bandsaw, or on a jigsaw this miniature coal will remove the teeth altogether.

188

Earliest dynamo fitted to a Royal Navy ship, HMS *Inflexible*, manufactured by the Brush Electric Company (exhibit at Portsmouth Historic Dockyard; picture and information courtesy of Mike Lee). One of the important innovations to the battleship HMS *Inflexible* in 1881 was the introduction of DC electricity, the earliest ship to be furnished with this luxury. Those who doubt this fact should be pointed in the direction of Portsmouth Historic Dockyard Museum in the UK, where the original 80V dynamo of this famous vessel is preserved. When she was sold for scrap at Chatham in 1903, someone had the foresight to keep this classic piece of early electric generation, before the rest of the ship was cut to pieces. The Brush Dynamo Company had already proved its worth and reliability at Messrs John Elder & Co, as working examples of this electrical generator were in constant use in their Glasgow factory where they had a reputation for reliability and performance. John Elder's firm were well established and famous for their development of the compound steam engine, as fitted in triple inverted form, to *Inflexible* and in its much simpler form, the type of horizontal engine installed into *Gannet*, but in her particular case, manufactured by Humphrys Tennant & Co at their Deptford works. My first question regarding *Inflexible* is 'What was the electricity generated for?' The quick answer is mainly for lighting and powering the searchlights; these new wonders quickly acquired the nickname of the 'Englishman's midnight sun'. At this time in history, Swan/Edison's incandescent light bulb had recently been perfected, which for ships large and important enough to carry dynamos was a huge leap forward in terms of convenience and safety. To put this in a commercial context, this was five years before the

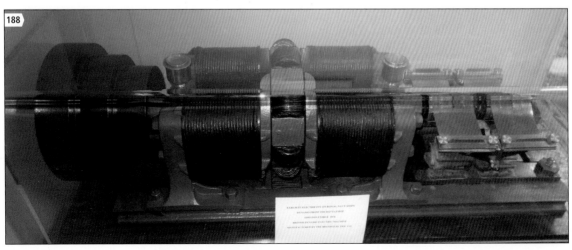

lighting of the Savoy Theatre in London, the first theatre in the world to be lit entirely by electric light in 1881. Like ships, theatres were victims of naked flames and caught fire with great regularity. They were totally transformed by the new invention. Those of us now used to flicking a light switch ought always to remember that electricity has to have a power source to generate it, and at this time that flow of current was derived from a constantly attended auxiliary steam engine, driven by coal, both on land and by sea. Fire and naked flame is, and was always, a constant cause for concern aboard ship, and these coal-bearing ships were prone to all kinds of ignition sources from wax candles, dripping oil lamps, the spark of a tinderbox, but most likely of all, badly stowed self-igniting coal, especially in the tropics. If ships' bunkers were not properly ventilated, the outbreak of fire was an ever present possibility because of the build-up of gas fumes, and this was the most feared source of alarm. The gun vessel HMS *Doterel*, the name vessel of this whole group of gunships, sank after an explosion while passing through the Straits of Magellan in 1881, caused by the ignition of gas in the ships' bunkers. Ridding ships of wax candles and oil-burning lamps meant that this particular source of naked flame was extinguished. It did not, however, mean the end of furnace fires and glowing embers, sparks from gun barrels and red-hot shot or even the humble clay-pipe accidentally knocked out on the cabin floor whilst still alight.

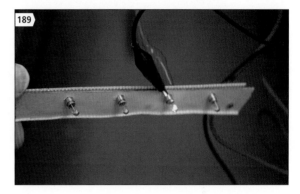

189

Rank of miniature incandescent light bulbs, placed under the coal shelves above the model engine and boilers. Apart from electrical apparatus for detonating the spar torpedoes, *Gannet* was almost certainly not fitted with any other electrical appliances for quite some while. Nevertheless, 12V DC incandescent bulbs are to be introduced to the model, and it is quite a thought that these bulbs have not changed in style or substance since the time they were first invented. Although they are miniatures, they still have a filament, a glass dome and are filled with an inert gas, in whose vacuum the filament glows and provides the light. The official title at supplier Maplin UK is LES lamp 12V and matching lamp holder BU14 & UJ72. The protrusion with the lamp fixed in the holder is 20mm, another important factor when fitting. There are shorter, rounder bulbs still made for this lamp-holder, but the longer storm-lantern shape looks just right, particularly on a low voltage setting. Light-emitting diodes are now all the rage in electronic devices, and are known to have a long life and the advantage of giving off low levels of heat; they are not, however, suited to giving ambient light, their forte being a focused spotlight, rather than the provision of side and overall light, such as is required to illuminate the inside of a cabin. My real objection to them is that they cannot, at their present stage of development, give that 'oily' appearance of low light which is so reminiscent of ship's DC lighting and glowing filaments. Incandescent bulbs are not so sensitive to electric current in the same way as LEDs, with the advantage that with these bulbs, it is easy to reduce the voltage to dim the lights and also replace the bulbs in their sockets. This reduction of voltage is important if the displayed model is on show for any length of time; by reducing the transformer from 9V to 6V output, the heat given off by the bulbs is small, yet the model still looks as she should in terms of illumination. If you reduce or increase the voltage of an LED beyond its specification, it will either not work at all, or it may burn out. Sometimes they can even change colour! A 12V DC transformer is required to power up the lighting circuit from AC mains electricity, and it is very useful to have the sort which has a variable stepped output, which many of them do these days. The one in use here is 240/50Hz, rated at 3A output (L10BR, Maplin UK). It is powering a total of thirty-two bulbs, well within its capability. On the *Gannet* model, there is to be a shelf fitted either side of the ship's interior walls, on the top of which lies a layer of miniature coal. On the underside, a rank of lights is wired to illuminate the engine and boiler spaces. This produces an issue of heat dispersal and reflection, not serious in this particular case, because they are not being fitted to an enclosed space, and a simple coat of white paint acts as a reflector to make the light source as bright as possible. Silver paper or a more efficient means of reflecting light can be used, but remember that all metal has the ability to conduct electricity, and if the positive pole for some unguarded reason hits the tinfoil, you will fuse the circuit. Wiring it up is simple enough. These bulbs work in parallel, that is to say you have two wires, a positive and a negative, and so long as the negative wire is connected to the lamp socket holders correctly, and the positive wire is connected to the positive wing on top of the lamp holder, all will be well. The socket holders have little metal wings with positive and negative tags, to avoid any confusion, so even for the complete tyro this is not a difficult wiring-up job. Within reason, a great many bulbs can be wired up to the same circuit; it all depends on the output of the transformer. Wired up like this, it doesn't matter if one of the light bulbs fails, the circuit will not be broken; this is another big advantage, particularly where access is hard to gain quickly to a failed bulb.

190

191

Junction box made for the wiring.
Wiring, even though it is in very small
gauge, needs to be hidden away, but
the junction box must have sufficient
length left on it for repairs to be carried
outside the hull in the event of failure.
The whole loom of wiring may need
attention and, for convenience, this has
to happen over the side of the model,
so the junction box cannot be flush-
fitted, and has to have enough slack on
it to be taken under the lower deck and
hidden away. When the full-sized
Warrior was wired up for the
restoration programme in the 1990s,
orders were given that no anachronistic
wiring should show where the public
would see it. In practice, this is very
hard to achieve, both in full scale and
in a model; the electrical circuit needs
to be carefully thought out to avoid
exposed wiring.

Miniature coal shelves. The wiring is done in parallel. The miniature coal is held
together by mixing it up with neat wood glue, arranging it into a drift and then
allowing it to dry; it is then resprayed with satin black paint. Note how the wiring
is fixed in parallel – the red wire is the positive, the green wire is the negative. It is
important that this shelf can be accessed in the case of bulb failure, so it has to be
bolted to the underside of the main deck, and note that the shelf is sufficiently
wide to shield the bulbs beneath. When lighting an area, you cannot have
protruding light bulbs which dazzle the onlooker (and also a camera), so it is
important to check the sightlines of any such fittings from all angles and make
sure they are shaded correctly. The bulb deck beams, which had some time ago to
be cut away in order to gain access to a major part of the hull, were put to one
side, and can now be reintroduced as the lampshades for the interior cabin
lighting. There is not a great deal of height under the deck beams so a snug fit is to
be encouraged, and adopting the identical roof camber is the most efficient way of
doing this. The lights in the cabins have been fixed in place with nuts and bolts,
which have the advantage that all the units are, with some difficulty, removable for
bulb replacement.

192

Light-box. Experimenting with a light-box and coal effect.
Embers and ash from any fire grate have a diffused and spent
look, very different from the oxygenated fire grate of a
working boiler, glowing fiercely with orange to white heat.
Various experiments on the model were tried to get this
ashen effect, ending with some dry,
grey-coloured tape, which I think
originated as a section of glassfibre
tape. Any fine-grained mesh would give
this look, and it occurs to me a similar
effect could be achieved with fine 14pt
embroidery fabric. It is important for
the chosen material to breathe and
disperse the heat of the miniature bulbs
beneath, and also let out some light at
the top and bottom. The fact that it is

fitted with three flicker bulbs does make it look very real,
and it also gives a sensation of movement in the shadows it
casts around the boiler room floor. The copper and brass
fittings on the boiler back heads also glint as an added
bonus.

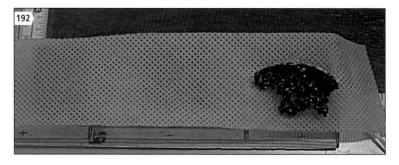

193

Red-hot ash. Light-box placed in front of the engine, with the addition of a coal drift, giving the effect of hot coals raked out from the boiler ash pans. Anyone prepared to travel, and wishing to see a truly effective full-sized diorama of a working boiler space in full scale, should take a trip to see the stunning exhibit aboard the preserved ss *Great Britain* (1843) at Bristol in the UK. I have tried my best to copy what they have done, but for an experience of how it must have felt aboard ship in the stokehold of one of these early hybrid vessels, complete with sight and surround sound, I can heartily recommend this re-creation. It is only one of the many excitements of how the restoration of *Great Britain* has been treated, but it is an example to all the others.

194

Cable deck illuminated for the first time, showing the detail of the 64pdr bow-chaser gun.

195

Engine room view of the stokehold.

196

Boiler back heads: view from the mainmast housing. Note the miniature storm lantern bulbs.

RUNNING LIGHTS

The Admiralty considered the navigation lights of a ship to be of extreme importance, and 'Regulations for preventing collisions at sea' had a direct bearing on where the running lights were placed and how they were lit. Mr Gray's poem was learned and used by every seaman on duty watch:

Meeting steamers do not dread
When you see three lights ahead:
Port your helm and show your red.
Green to green or red to red;
Perfectly safe, go ahead.
If to starboard red appear
'Tis your duty to keep clear;
To act as judgement says is proper:
Port, or Starboard, Back or stop her.
But when upon your port is seen
A steamer's starboard light of green,
There's not so much for you to do,
For green to port keeps clear of you.
Both in safety, and in doubt
Always keep a good look out;
In danger with no room to turn
Ease her, stop her, go astern.

197

Overhead the engine room and stokehold; note the boilers now have steam domes and valves fitted.

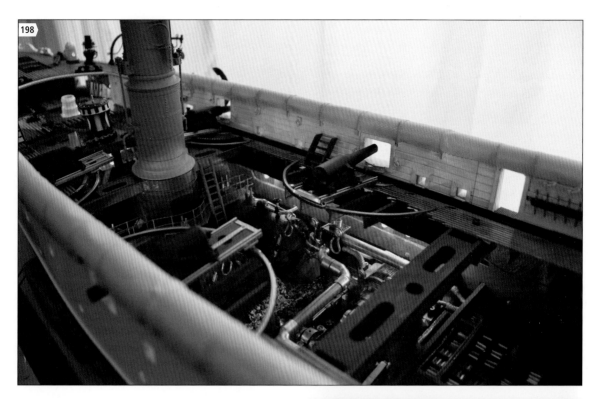

198

Theatrical effect of internal lighting brings all the below-deck detail alive.

199

Running lights: the above-decks illumination with fully enclosed helmet style of port-side bow light. On the model, the raw material for this bullet-shaped lantern originally came from two discarded miniature 90cwt gun castings, whose firing chambers were parted from their barrels, put in the lathe chuck, bored out and shaped. They could easily have been made from capped-off tube, but metal is important to counteract the blistering build-up of heat from any enclosed incandescent bulb. They really do get hot. The 'helmet' style for bow lights had been popularised by long voyages made with clipper-ship bows; a fine entry meant that this quarter of the ship spent much of her time plunging her nose, creating difficulties when trying to keep a light source from being doused, be it oil- or candle-powered. It also ensured a degree of safety, in that the naked flame was totally enclosed and the helmet was permanently fixed to the deck, rather than being suspended or attached to the standing rigging. Access to these fittings was from the deck below, so that they could be made externally watertight, and serviced immediately there was a problem of any kind. When is a sailing ship not a sailing ship? As far as the Admiralty were concerned, sailing ships and steamers were considered as follows: 'Every steam vessel which is under sail and not under steam is to be considered a sailing vessel, and every

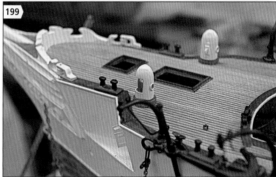

vessel under steam, whether under sail or not, is to be considered a steam vessel.' This rule, under 'Preliminary Regulations', affected the position of lights and how many running lights were carried; the length of the vessel was also important, and *Gannet*, when riding at anchor, and being over 150ft in length, would have shown two lights on the foremast with at least 15ft separating them. These upper white lights had a wider arc of 12 points of the compass rather than the 10 points of the side lamps. The angle of the bow light was also laid down in statute as follows: 'On the portside, a red light so constructed as to show an unbroken light over the arc of the horizon 10 points of the compass, so fixed as to throw the light from right ahead to two points abaft the beam on the port side and of such a character as to be visible at a distance of at least two miles.' This order was mirrored for the green glass of the starboard light.

200

Fenestrating the window of the port-side bow light with a miniature diamond-coated disc. The only difficulty is cutting out a rectangular shape of 112 degrees to give the required angle of light. Cross-cutting the tube is easy enough, but tackling the uprights either means drilling through and filing out, or the freehand use of the diamond grit wheel in the angle drill, which requires courage. White metal is very sticky, so the object was loaded onto a section of dowelling, clamped in a vice and, importantly, with good right-arm support, the diamond cutting wheel on slow revs did the work (Dremel wheel). The coloured inserts of plastic (made from ballpoint pen holders) reach only halfway up the inserted inner plastic glass, thus allowing heat to escape. Light will always pick up colour, so this makes little difference in practice, although it does not meet Admiralty instructions.

201

Mushroom-headed helm compass under construction. The ship's compass is detailed on the plan atop the tall column. Compasses at sea have presented all kinds of problems to navigators and helmsmen ever since the discovery of magnetic north. By the 1870s these delicate instruments, which were vital in every way for successful navigation, had reached new levels of accuracy, thanks to the innovative mind of Sir William Thompson, later Lord Kelvin (1824–1907). But they were still exposed to extremes of hot sunshine on a sunny day, as well as freezing temperatures at night. Swollen seas often drenched them, condensation caused by temperature changes from night to day meant internal moisture dripping onto the compass card, and worse still, salt-sea air would have unmercifully corroded the delicate compensating magnets surrounding the rim of the compass card. To operate efficiently, the prime requisite for a compass bowl is that the card to has remain level, whilst the supporting binnacle beneath it pitches, tosses and rolls with the movement of the ship. Added to this problem was how to illuminate them adequately at night and also read the compass bearing accurately through the new addition of the azimuth prism. Other issues included the proximity of such things as the iron frames of the ship's structure, and the magnetic deviations caused by dense lumps of iron and steel from which the guns and their barrels were made. Further complications were caused by the issue of how best to balance the magnetism of the compass card itself within the hood. Note also on this particular ship how the helm compass is in absolute parallel with the two 5in Vavasseur CP guns, mounted on the sponsons; these guns had long barrels which were constantly following targets and must have severely affected the localised magnetic field.

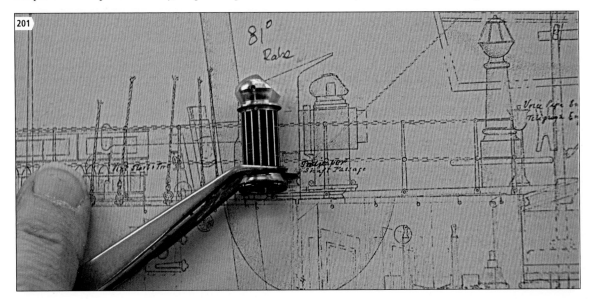

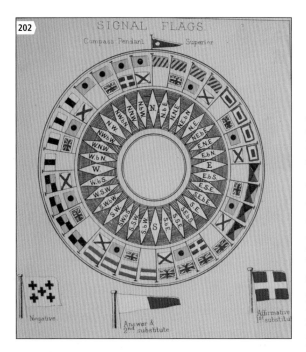

202

Compass card and signal flags. The mushroom-headed compass was the very latest navigational aid. The description given in Nare's 1897 manual of seamanship is very thorough:

> The compass card consists of a central aluminium boss and an outer aluminium rim connected together by fine silk cords. Small magnets from two or three inches long are suspended from the rim by silk cords, and thin paper marked with the points of the compass and degrees is attached to the rim and partially supported by the silk cords between the rim and the boss. The paper ring is cut across in thirty two places, midway between the silk thread spokes, to prevent it from warping the aluminium ring by the shrinkage it experiences when heated by the sun. By this arrangement the principal part of the weight is in the rim, and is consequently as far as possible from the centre on which the card moves. This gives a very long period of free oscillation, which, from mathematical reasoning, is known to give great steadiness. The central aluminium boss has a hole in its centre which rests on the projecting

lip of a small inverted aluminium cup ... which rests on a fixed iridium point. With the small needles of this card the complete application of the principles of correction is easy and sure. To correct the quadrantal error a pair of hollow iron globes is used: one globe is placed on each side of the compass on a convenient support.

Should anyone wish to view the compass and compass card of Sir William Thomson, the Discovery Point Museum at Dundee, Scotland, not only has Scott's ship on display, but also the original compass used on the first exploration voyage (1901), in their wonderful display of all things Antarctic, based on Scott's two Antarctic journeys (1901 and 1911), the first of which was, as far as the Royal Navy was concerned, trying to understand the behaviour of magnetism in the high latitude of the South Pole. This is yet another detail which links HMS *Gannet* historically with SS *Discovery*. The binnacle of any compass is, in reality, a circular supporting wooden cupboard in which all the small items necessary for interpreting the navigational charts are kept. Binnacles are made from wood and brass to insulate them from any effects of localised magnetism, and their construction avoids any kind of magnetic material; they house the precious charts, keeping them both handy and dry. Because binnacles are placed on open decks more often than not in reality, the tongue and groove construction of the cupboard allowed the mahogany timber to expand and contract in sunshine and rain, without developing cracks and shakes in the structure. Perversely, the model binnacle is made from brass, and the process begins by etching the grooves of the binnacle with the parting-off tool on the cross slide of the lathe, moving it by hand with the lathe slide's hand wheel, with brass bar loaded into the lathe chuck. The twelve divisions of the binnacle column are controlled by marking up the bull wheel gear of the lathe with white spots, and using a wooden spatula as a detente. Before any piercing procedure takes place on the model dome head, the face is presented to the revolving strap of the linisher, loaded tightly onto a dowel stick, carefully marked, and placed in a 'V'-groove machine block at a 55-degree angle, before grinding off its face. A bit of practice is advised, because you only get one chance to carry out this operation of producing a flat face to the machined surface of the dome, but this is how it was done for the model.

203

Linishing off the face of the mushroom held against the revolving strap. Note the use of the engineer's 'V'-block. Brass is used so that the mushroom head of the compass can be carefully bored out and the domed head of the compass subsequently pierced through with a dental burr when the item has been transferred to the milling machine; note that the head of the dome is slightly wider than the binnacle. This extra width of the dome gives the opportunity to machine its widened mouth by moving the milling table on the A/B axis – in and out, in other words – but only fractionally. An ellipse is a difficult shape to reproduce, but in reality allows for a larger compass card to be fitted and illuminated; the larger the circumference of the card, the steadier it becomes, and this added stability makes it easier for accurate bearings to be taken and followed, especially after nightfall.

204

Helm furnishings. In the centre, mounted on the raised platform, are the details of the ship's compass, voice pipes and engine telegraph, all encircled by the stanchion rail; sited aft, the mushroom-headed helm compass, now completed with soft iron spheres and a Flinder's bar with a second engine telegraph near at hand and a 'syren', as it is described on the plan. Further attachments to complete the detail of the helm compass head include candleholders, compass card, and a drop handle for the binnacle cupboard door.

ADMIRALTY SPECIFICATIONS No. 155, VOICE PIPES AND TELEGRAPHS

The voice pipes are to be made of copper, with mouth pieces, whistles, stop-cocks, and wire gauze diaphragms where necessary, and to be fitted wherever directed. The pipes to be cased. Care is to be taken to break the continuity of copper pipes, in order that they shall not be conductors of lightning to the magazine. The Engine Contractor will provide and fit engine room telegraphs and voice pipes from the bridge to the engine room.

205

Wardroom furnishings. Commander's bed space, sectioned off the wardroom with removable panelling, receiving the finishing touches by members of the restoration team in a Nielsen photograph from 25 September 2003. By 1885 linoleum flooring was commonly being fitted to the floors of wardrooms in the navy. It was a new material invented some thirty years previously from experiments with a hot process, solidifying linseed oil laid onto canvas, and it meant that not only was it strikingly different from ship's decking, but also very practical where salt-laden sea boots and extremes of weather were concerned, to say nothing of crumbs fallen from the table and sticky spills from drinking. Hygiene was by now well understood in the Navy as being both smart and practical. Rats, however, were still a common fact of life.

206

Captain's table. A Nielsen archive photograph of the beautifully French-polished mahogany table, specially constructed to the ship's plans; in the background, also to the specifications of the original 1885 plans, is the buffet/canteen surrounding the mizzenmast. In peacetime the captain's table had a dual role. Its highly polished surface was covered with a green baize cloth on which the charts would be laid out in full, and courses plotted. It was sited immediately beneath the overhead skylight for this very purpose – daylight being important to see clearly all the detail contained on the charts, not only for plotting the course, but also taking note of the draught of water, tidal warnings and other natural hazards which might endanger the ship.

208

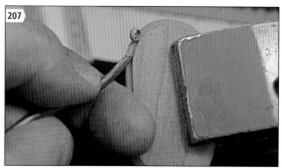

207

Miniature table top. A 2mm 'U' gauge being used to detail the table edging – a tricky moment where it goes against the grain. This was done freehand, having first sanded off the circumference of the table at a steep angle on the linisher. This gave a better surface for the gouge to bed into the walnut timber. I would only attempt this with a dense timber – mahogany has too open a grain for carving at this scale to be successfully carried out; fruit-wood or other choice timbers of that nature would be advised. The joints for the sub-frame of the table are made with the bandsaw blade kerf, before the turning process begins. The miniature table legs need to be turned at as fast a speed as possible (1500rpm) from square stock centred in a (four-jaw) chuck; the shape of the leg is derived from first sharpening a 'D' cutter bit and turning it at high speed. It helped to scale the look of the model table edge by slightly reducing the circumference, just leaving a narrow outer edge. It is not quite to scale, but it does convey that special carved end grain into which later applications of varnish sink, giving that subtle look of reality from using timber in the solid.

208

Chaises longues, luxuriously upholstered in plum-coloured velvet, photographed by Nielsens on 23 February 2006. Comfortable, upholstered seating in the modern sense is not a matter often discussed by naval historians concerned with nineteenth-century warships. Crew members had to make do with simply a three-legged stool, a bench or a hammock; there was no concept of what we might think of as comfortable lounging, and precious little time for it either. This lack of modern-day luxury applied equally to commissioned officers, except for the commander's quarters, where he enjoyed the comparative comfort of a cot/bed. The sofas, or 'chaises longues', would have been reserved for guests, in the main, rather than the relaxation of senior officers. They are lovingly illustrated on the plan as deeply buttoned and plush fitted. Claret-coloured velvet has been used by Nielsen's restoration team, and they do look wonderful, although I have a suspicion that the originals were more likely finished in leather, which is a more practical and hard-wearing material where moisture and seawater are concerned.

209

Seating (model). Well-used-looking upholstery after a few years at sea – a model interpretation. The cushioning effect in resin putty is made with the impress of a miniature cross-headed screwdriver, and the legs, which are to follow, will be made from copper wire.

210

Commander's cot/bunk, drawer unit and wash bowl. These are all detailed from the ship's plans. The commander's bunk-bed, drawer unit and washbasin stand are wonderful examples of slightly curved built-in furniture, designed to use every last square inch of space against the hull interior. It is still a concept with which we are familiar today in youngsters' bedrooms, where a host of small items can be kept tidily in drawers, whilst the occupant sleeps soundly on the top of the unit, in this case fitted with traditional wooden rails to hold the bedding and the sleeper safely in place. In this extract from his memoirs of his experiences aboard a similar vessel to

Gannet in 1885, HMS *Woodlark* stationed in Rangoon, Admiral George Ballard gives a glimpse of what life was like in the wardroom of a typical gun vessel:

A sudden change of ship in those days involved a great deal more in the way of personal inconvenience and expense to an officer than it does now because the only cabin fittings supplied by the Admiralty were a chest of drawers, a chair and a bunk. Everything else, including bedding, blankets, bath, water cans, wash-hand basin, looking-glass, carpet, curtains etc. had to be provided by each officer

for himself ... for her size the ship was not uncomfortable but I had the smallest of the cabins as the junior lieutenant and standing in the doorway I could reach out far enough to touch the ship's side over the bunk. Under the bunk were the naval drawers, but to open these I had to back out of the door. In the space between the bunk and the cabin bulkhead which separated it from the wardroom, there was just room for a chair at one end and a narrow wash stand at the other; I was obliged to have my morning tub in the wardroom ...

211

Miniature stove. Fire doors for the miniature stove, made with a square punch into a block of hardwood. It is perhaps fitting that the last domestic item to be modelled in the wardroom is the stove. It is not known exactly what type of stove kept this quarter of the ship snug and warm, but I have copied a French

ADMIRALTY SPECIFICATIONS No. 160

Cabin furniture; the cabins are to be fitted complete with all bed-places, cots, drawers, book shelves, hat and coat pegs, tables, wash and other stands, shelves, sideboards, lockers and all other fittings (exclusive of bedding and other upholstery) complete in every respect, agreeably to the practice in HM Service for ships of this class, and as may be directed by the Overseer.

stove, with its highly decorated and embossed sweeps and adornments. The technical name for this kind of extravagant style is neo-rococo or late baroque. Given that the fire doors containing the flickering flames would be the centrepiece of the wardroom furnishings, in quiet moments there would be plenty of carved detail to look at and study. This French style of stove was fitted to SS *Discovery*, and given that she sailed under Royal Navy command, it is not unreasonable to guess that it was an imported item. The French firm Salamandre who supplied Scott's ship with four of them is still in production in Paris, and the restored wardroom of HMS *Warrior* has something a little larger, but very similar in style.

212

Wardroom stove
detailed with
ashpan and
chimney. (The
jeweller's anvil is
dated 1894 with
the Wilkinson's
scissors symbol.)
In terms of
design, the hood
of this stove is
very important

because it is rounded and it will therefore catch the light
when it is in position below the poop deck. The glazing-bar
frames have been punched into the end grain with a metal
punch, fashioned from sharpened square-section brass bar; a
few light taps is all that is required, and punching has the
advantage that it crushes the end grain of the wood at the
back of the frame, and flattens it. The model stove was
sprayed all over with black satin paint and before the surface
had completely cured, it was quickly wiped over with a cloth
soaked in cellulose thinners to bring out the highlights of the
metal detail. This demonstrates the advantage of using
copper and brass; tackling it in this way gives the impression
that the stove is all one casting, rather than a mass of twisted
copper wire and shim, attached to the end of a block of
wood. To make sense of what is going on below in the
wardroom, the poop-deck stovepipe needs to coincide with
the fitting below. On the ship's plan, this pipe is stayed with
removable chain, for the practical reason that it interferes
with the propeller hoist and the spanker boom, and would
no doubt have been capped off and stowed away when the
ship was under sail.

213

Wardroom furnishings completed with linoleum-style
flooring, typical of the age. Can any of this be seen? Well
yes, it can: not what you would expect, but there are
glimpses of the sofa wings, the drawer unit, the stove, the
chart table and the chequered flooring, which reflects
light in a quite extraordinary way, with its shiny surface
derived from the use of photographic paper; this is a
welcome and unexpected bonus. It can all be seen
through the quarter-gallery lights as well as the side
ports, and in the age of the mobile-phone camera, there
is no hiding place.

214

Internal details of the model hull complete, and originally
the end of the story – but then came the irresistible urge to
step the three masts and rig the model.

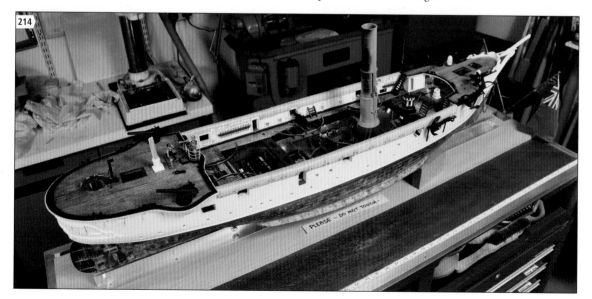

9: Masts and Spars

215

Lower yard. Here in the Nielsen's yard at Gloucester we see the lower yard in preparation, with added squared shoulders at the extremes (Nielsen photograph from 29 August 2002). The shoulders of the yards are made from oak, for the extra strength required by the sheave slots. The rest of the yard, made from Douglas fir, has been prepared with tapered 'eighth-squaring'.

216

Mast-making (model). Eighth-squaring the mainmast for the model. All HMS *Gannet*'s replacement masts and spars have been made from Douglas fir, the same species of timber used for her original masts and spars in 1878. The replacements from the Forest of Dean were seasoned in the mast pond for years before being squared and installed. Since the days of wooden walls, shipyard mast-making has always been revered as a separate and highly skilled trade, and with good reason. In manufacture, the most difficult aspect, in full scale and in miniature, is knowing where you are in terms of the dimensions of a bole of timber which is being tapered from square to round, but retaining squared features such as cheeks and tenon joints, which must lie with great accuracy in relation to the vessel below. The slightest variation or deviation from the horizontal or vertical will show, and this applies not only to the housing of the mast through the decks, but also to the fitting of the cross-trees, the fighting tops, the caps and the iron bands of the doublings, of which there will be more detail later. Douglas fir is my favourite timber for mast-making and as with the full-sized vessel, I have had some stock put by for a while. As a species it is stable, strong and flexible, but all timber on a sawn length has a slight bend which will always be detectable, so when matching timbers for mast-making it is a good idea to cancel out any warping tensions by clamping two lengths and gluing them together against their natural bias. This gives the added advantage of having a centre line on the end grain which will not disappear when the hand-planing process takes place, and you also retain a constant reference to that critical datum line. Another important tip is to grind the top end of the mast into a cone, leaving a pointed shape like that made by an old-fashioned pencil sharpener. This has three advantages – you retain the centre reference point, you can calculate with an o/s calliper the final width at the masthead, and it physically assists the hand plane with the evenness of the tapering process. Having established the dimensions of the mast, including the housing below decks, always allow an extra length of timber for hand-planing, providing yourself with a handgrip at the mast base; this will give you the ability to roll the mast as the hand-planing process takes place. At the end of the procedure, this extra length at the mast foot is removed. Why don't you use a lathe for making masts? Well, you can for the central bunt, but the one word 'whip' gives the game away; long thin lengths of timber will always produce whipping, whereas hand-planing on a bench gives support to the full length of the mast as the tapering process is taking place, thus giving an even and controlled diminish to the full length of the mast. Masts and yards should always start as squared timber; the first process is reduction by what is called eighth-squaring, a technique which mast- and yard-making requires; it simply means planing down the square edges of the stick and making eight flat, tapering and evenly spaced surfaces; make sure your plane blade is nice and sharp, but finish the process with a flat file followed by sanding. You will see from the pictures that I now use non-slip rubber matting when planing masts down. This is a relatively new product which I find enormously useful and, because it grips the total length of the mast during the process, it gives more control and there is less wrist effort required to achieve the final taper.

217

Machining the housing joint from the solid tree trunk at Gloucester docks, using a tethered chainsaw, with the bole of the tree running on a track beneath in a Nielsen photograph from 29 August 2002. The mast poles had spent years in the mast pond to season them, and produced a terrible stench when cut. The dramatic picture of the chainsaw at Nielsen's yard is an eye-opener in terms of overcoming a difficult procedure with a common power tool, but the same effect in miniature can be arrived at with the combined use of a bandsaw and engineer's 'V'-block. In order to make the first joint on the model at the masthead, which will house the cross-trees and chess-trees, a parallel saw-cut is made on both sides of the masthead, returning this section from round back into a square form.

218

Identical procedure in miniature, using a bandsaw in conjunction with an engineer's 'V'-block as a guide. Once again, the marked-up centre line is vital. When this cut has been made and trimmed, the trees and the fighting top will be able to slide into position. This joint has to be made carefully, so that the fighting top will sit fairly and squarely into the joint, but it must also allow for the compensating 6-degree angle of steeve, to be parallel with the waterline. The cheeks, or hounds, are then sited into the base of the cut and their top edges made to lie in the same plane as the deck. This is tricky to get right, and in my case these edges were machined on the table saw, using the mitre fence at the correct angle, after they were fixed in place, in order to get the top level at the right angle and an accurate seating for the chess-trees.

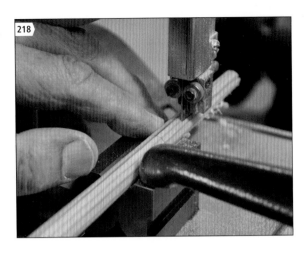

219

Squared masthead, chess-trees and cross-trees; the supporting side brackets are known as the hounds or bibs. The chess-trees are the forward-facing timbers which have the open mortise joint cut crosswise into them and are sturdier than the cross-trees which support the platform on the outer edges. In reality, the top has to be light enough for removal but strong enough to house the joint of the topmast(s) and in full size the weight of those marines who could well be using it for sniper fire in a battle situation or skirmish. These supporting timbers also provide for a series of eyebolts on their undersides, to which running tackle is attached.

220

Fighting top. Foremast, HMS *Gannet* restoration, 19 August 2013. The fighting top also has an extra role to play as a spreader for the futtock chains which support the deadeyes of the rigged topmast above. The top is a complicated detail to get right, and at this late stage of the sailing navy it changes from being the shape of a 'D' into more of a pointed arrow. The reason for this development is to allow the top yards a greater arc of travel, with the topmast shrouds swept back in line with the masthead. All these details need to be drawn up on the board with some accuracy in order for the fighting top to fulfil all its roles and be a success. The improvements in design allowed the ship to be sailed closer to the wind.

221

Fighting top (model) under construction. The top rim which surrounds the top is of the greatest importance in terms of strength and stability – even in model form – because of the strains which can be exerted on the platform by the tension of the topmast rigging. The 'D'-shaped banding, made from beech dowel planed in half, is glued and clamped very firmly to the outer edge, having first been steamed into shape on the heated copper tube; this will prevent the total platform from warping, a sight sometimes seen on older models where the rigging has shrunk or been made too taut, pulling the fighting top unwillingly into the shape of a bowler-hat rim. On the model, the top has initially been made from two layers of ply, followed by two layers of paper – the upper one marked with the detailed drawing of

the construction, and the lower one blank, but counteracting the glued surface above. Failure to do this gluing on both sides will introduce warping; all layers of glue in a veneering situation must be balanced up, or it will create distortion. Planking on the fighting tops is so arranged that it not only gives the strongest possible support to the structure surrounding the trestle-trees, but also provides a sure grip for the barefooted crew, whose feet will always lie across the grain on the outer edges. A fighting top is well drained, but potentially presents a very hazardous and slippery position aloft. Normally, a safety rail would be fitted to the forward rim of the top, but in reality and in practice this would cause chafing to the foot of the topsails, and a stanchion rail would soon rip the foot rope and canvas cloth to shreds.

222

Drawing board: details of the bowsprit spike, masts, spars and fittings transferred to the drawing board. Because all the yards, booms, gaffs and spars of a ship play separate individual roles, and they all differ from one another, it is a good idea to sort them out on paper, with all their fittings, before manufacturing them. This is time-consuming, but still the fastest way in the end, because it is vital that they all fit together and no detail is missed before it becomes too difficult to rectify. The dimensions have been taken from the 1:192 illustration of HMS *Gannet* by Medway College, laid down in preparation for the ship's restoration. The measurements have been converted into 1:48 scale or one quarter of an inch to the foot. As to their interpretation when being modelled, try and keep all the dimensions to the leanest interpretation possible. Always bear in mind that any item to do with wooden spars on a ship requires manhandling at sea, either being sent down or hoisted aloft.

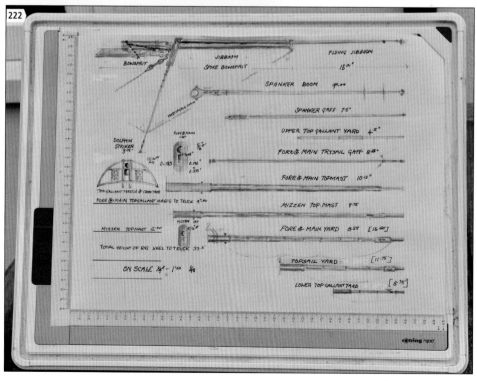

223

Assembly of the spike bowsprit (bowsprit, jibboom and flying jibboom). Note also the heel chain and the crupper chain. The spike bowsprit is how the three spars at the forefront of the rigging are described. The strength provided by the heel of the bowsprit and its housing takes the majority of the strain exerted by the outer rigging, as well as supporting any back or side strain pulling on the foremast. It is firmly stayed to the ship's hull with back guys and on its underside, by the bobstay chain.

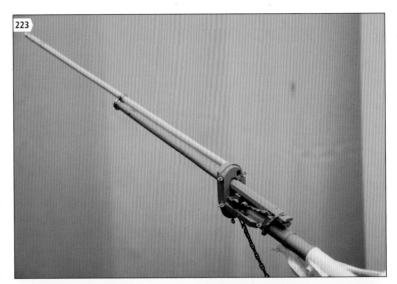

224

Bowsprit cap under construction for the model. In full size, the bowsprit and the cap are fixed – the booms can be run in and out. The bowsprit cap is filed through at an angle and then banded for strength, which will present an issue if it does not have a grooved seating around its circumference. This is because it is the shape of a collar with a raked angle forward, and it will not lie happily without a deep channel at the head and foot of it. On the model the iron band should really be made of brass strip, but 1.25mm copper wire is always more forgiving and can be lightly hammered into position to gain the same effect.

225

The banding groove of the bowsprit cap, rotated by hand on the milling table. In full size, it was iron-banded for strength. The other two forward-facing poles of the spike, the jibboom and the flying jibboom can be unshipped as with any topmast, but the bowsprit and the wooden cap remain as permanent fixtures. The detail of the heel chain and crupper chain are standard fitments for a RN ship of this period. The crupper chain passes through a shallow angled sheave slot at the foot of the boom, tensioned up (bowsed) on the port side with lanyards riven through deadeye blocks. The crupper chain secures the inner end of the boom close down onto the saddle. The whole spike is steeved up on *Gannet* to the angle where the cap lies at 90 degrees to the water level. The jackstaff will eventually be secured to the cap with its tubular holder on the starboard side; it is always preferable to have any flagpole or banner flying horizontally, and a jackstaff fixed to a bowsprit cap always aims for this, a practice followed by all world navies.

226

Spike bowsprit rigging (model). The three poles projecting from the bowsprit cap are nominated the dolphin striker and port and starboard spritsail gaffs. The heavy chain beneath the bowsprit is the bobstay, tensioned by large heart blocks; the lighter chain supporting the jibboom is the martingale. The dolphin striker and martingale have back guys rigged, and the bobstay chain is tensioned by two heavily lashed heart blocks attached to an iron collar just aft the bowsprit end. The round turns riven through the heart blocks are still officially known as lanyards, and are easier to adjust than standard three-holed deadeyes. The dolphin striker primarily provides back tension for the jibboom, and it is modelled with a harpoon at its extremity; sited just above the harpoon are two downward-facing cleats on either side of the spike for the upper forestays to pass through on their journey to the outer walls of the ship's head. The lighter weight chain is referred to as the martingale and is tensioned by the back guys or back ropes. The whisker poles are so called, because the back ropes were in former times attached to the cathead – thus 'cat's whiskers', which is one way of describing the majestic appearance of the whole contrivance. The boom for the dolphin striker and also the whisker poles were all in former times attached to the bowsprit with a gaff jaw apiece, but in the latter days of sailing warships they are simply eye-bolted to the cap rather than rigged, suspended by the lifts.

227

Rigging the whisker poles, at considerable risk – a Nielsen photograph from 9 July 2003. The throat seizings of the back guys and lifts are being malleted onto the extremes of the whisker poles with a rubber mallet. Note the roping is all served (see below under rigging).

228

Model detail of whisker poles. All rigging lines, both in full scale and miniature, need tensioning carefully because there is a totality which has to be achieved if none of the lines is to go slack. This interdependence means fitting thimbles to every line of rigging, which can be adjusted as each new rope is added. Fortunately, what works in full scale also replicates in miniature, and three turns of a miniature rope through a thimble or shackle will tension or slacken each line, giving the possibility of readjustment at all times. If a line does go slack or is in some way snagged, it is a quick job to cut through the lanyard section, and reapply the tension, 'bowsed in' is the old-fashioned term, without having to remake the whole rope.

229

Topmast. The untreated timber of the model's topmast is stepped through to the mainmast below, housed tightly between the trestle-trees and the cross-trees. Note the tenon joint at the main masthead, ready to receive the mast cap. The procedure for making these differs slightly from the lower masts, but most vital of all is the need to machine the squared mast foot before any other work is done; this is why it is always important to start with squared timber, even though masts are generally thought of as being round. A square cut at the head and the foot will ensure parallel alignment when they come to be fitted in the trestle-trees and the mast cap. It is also traditional to have the section between the fighting top and the lower cap as eighth-squared timber and a sheave slot cut, for hoisting the mast out of its housing; this runs in alignment, diagonally across the mast foot, just above the squared hole for the fid pin. There are two reasons for eighth-squaring in full-size practice, one is to produce a surface around which the bight of a rope or chain has grip – this particularly applies to the central portion of a yard, known as the bunt, around which the chain slings are rigged; the other is for gripping the foot of a topmast when it is being hauled out of its housing via an eyebolt fixed under the supporting cap above; this enables crew members to have the topmast sent down onto the deck, a most difficult and hazardous operation which was occasionally necessary. On the model, after the eighth-squaring of the bunt has been hand-filed, I removed a band width of approximately 2in with a file, so that I could get a small hand plane in the gap to start the tapering process of the mast, finishing it down with a flat diamond-coated file (Permagrit fine) and, finally, a sponge-backed abrasive.

230

Mast cap under construction. Note that the underlying wedge gives the angle (84 degrees) at which the housing slot must be cut. This angle allows the cap to run parallel with the waterline, counteracting the rake of the mast. Caps are difficult to get absolutely right; the issue has to do with boring out and accurately filing a squared hole at an angle to receive the masthead, with a round hole for the topmast almost immediately in front of it. Masts of this period are set with only the smallest gap possible between the doublings, just sufficient space for the standing rigging to be riven through the gap, which is why the square and the round hole almost touch. The included angle in this case is 84 degrees, and the 6-degree slope will ensure that the mast cap runs parallel to the waterline, and a tight fit in the tenon housing joint. These two cuts have to be made with enough accuracy in vertical alignment to include a tight push-fit onto the tenon of the masthead, and a push-fit above the eighth-squaring of the topmast. Any slight deviation of these piercings will give a misaligned result. The cap is only a small item and very prone to splitting, which is why in full scale it is iron-banded. Even with a model it needs to be made from a reliable hardwood – preferably boxwood, or any close-grained wood such as maple, beech or walnut, but not mahogany, which easily splits. It must be made removable because when it comes to the primary rigging it makes life a lot easier. The way to ensure a correct alignment to the cap joint angle is to carefully cut a small wedge from scrap wood, with a 6-degree angle, and use it as a sub-support to go underneath the strip of timber prepared for the cap and clamped up in the machine vice. This supporting wedge needs to be marginally thinner in section than the length of prepared timber, so that the vice jaws grip the piece to be machined. All five caps can then be initially clamped and drilled through with a pillar-drill support. The slot for mine is being milled out, having previously chain-drilled it for clearance to the milling bit, but the most important consideration is the wedge itself, rather than how it is bored out, because the procedure will anyway have to be finished off later with a small, squared, hand file. The first two caps for the fore- and mainmast came out well; that for the mizzen took three attempts to get it right – the first one had a split from the mast hole being too tight and the second a misalignment with the small mortise joint, both errors being a reminder of just how careful you have to be with this challenging job. The rewards, however, are the dramatic way in which topmasts heighten the stature of the model and give a certain degree of bravura to the whole project.

231

Topmast heel. This gives support to fitting the topmast top which follows shortly. This refers to the eighth-squared shoulder which has to be modelled in the only way I know how, which is to bore out a separate piece of squared timber and sleeve into position. When the glue is well cured, it is then filed down to give eight equally spaced faces, starting by taking off the corners of the square until they all meet with equal faces. This is easier to do when the section is firmly glued to the mast, but it is a good idea to protect the collar with a twist of tape or the file may damage the joint. In full scale, the heel gives a slightly increased area for seating the topgallant trestle-trees without adding greatly to the weight of the mast.

232

Topmast top. This item allows for spreading the topgallant backstays, and is somewhat fragile in full scale and miniature. In line with *Gannet*'s original rig as a barque (she has been restored as a fully rigged ship), this semi-circular platform appears only on the fore- and mainmasts and looks at first glance to be no more than a mast spreader, but there is more to it than that. The outer hoop and two curved mast spreaders aft, still referred to as cross-trees, have to be made with maximum strength, so spruce wood is steamed round a hot copper tube for the curvature, with two thicknesses of thin strip timber in tandem; wood glue is then applied between the plies of wood and clamped together with clips.

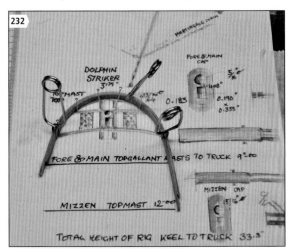

233

The foot of the topgallant mast housed into the topmast top. The cap has yet to be made. This makes for a surprisingly strong structure, to which the supporting chess-trees are then added on the underside; these need careful alignment before the adhesive is applied to ensure that the topgallant mast hole and the topmast head align. The next process is to glue the completed item to the eighth-squared topmast heel, remembering to set a 6-degree forward rake to match the lower masting systems. The advice here would be that the final process needs carrying out with the whole masting system erected on the model to check both vertical and horizontal alignment.

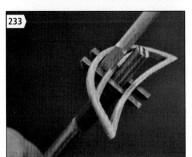

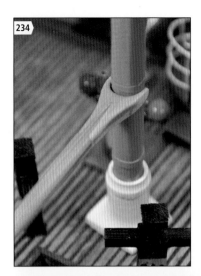

234

Spanker boom attaches to the mizzenmast; note the deep 'V' joint, typical of the jaw fitting of a gaff sail. It is always strengthened by banding. The long spanker boom overhangs the stern of the ship and is one of the considerations to be taken into account when measuring any model for its extreme dimensions. The perpendicular length of a vessel only includes the length of the wetted area of the hull and does not include the extra length added by a bowsprit, the upward curve of the stem-post or an overhung stern, so display-case makers beware. The jaw of the spanker boom consists of an iron-bound scarfed joint, the mouth of which rests on a collar attached to the mizzenmast. It is joined to the mast with a necklace of wooden balls, known as parrels, riven through with rope, allowing it to swing with ease around the mast collar. As with the mast tops, make sure that the collar has a 6-degree steeve to it, so that the jaw of the boom runs parallel with the waterline. The spanker gaff is made in a similar way to the boom, with an increased angle to the sliding jaw and fitted also with parrels. I am not planning to fit trysail gaffs to the fore- and mainmasts, intending to minimise any interference with viewing the internal detail.

235

Full-sized fore and main yards finished in the round at Gloucester Docks in a Nielsen photograph from 22 October 2002; note the bunt at the centre of the yard, and in the background, a tree trunk awaits further machining.

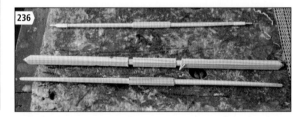

236

Three stages of miniature yard-making. In the picture the top yard is almost complete with shoulder sheaves added; the middle one is at a preliminary stage, the ends have been ground into cone shapes and the bunt (middle section) has yet to be eighth-squared; the measured depth of the cut in the slots allows for a file to be introduced, followed by a knuckle plane for finishing off. The forward yard in the picture is planed off, but still requires the squared section of shoulder sheaves to be added as described below. This first move is best judged by starting the process with an offcut from the original identical section, entering the experimental piece into the four-jaw chuck of the lathe, and depth measurements being taken and noted. It is important to get a sharp shoulder on the central bunt of the yard, and clear a width on either side of the bunt so that a hand file, followed by a small knuckle plane, can then be used in the gap created for it, and start the tapering process. Make sure the depth of cut is sufficient to be able to plane off the eight faces of the bunt representing the central battens of the mast. In full-scale practice, extra planks were often added over the eighth-squaring to prevent chafing from the chain slings and provide a larger diameter of grip.

237

Milling out the shoulder-sheave to receive a sheave (wheel). Slot-cutting can be done largely by hand, by chain-drilling with a 1mm drill and then chiselling out from both sides to prevent breakout. Even when using a miller bit, start with a preparatory drilling through, preceding the use of the milling cutter; small milling burrs and cutters will break if they do not have any previous clearance provided; it puts too great a strain on the cutter shank and the slot will wander off centre if no pilot holes for clearance have been drilled through it previously. The squared shoulder-sheave fittings to the ship's yardarms are unusual and not all that easy to make. By the final days of the sailing navy, timber yards on smaller fighting ships had become so slender and reliant on iron hoops for their strength that they needed extra width at their extremes for the sheaves to be fitted to the yardarms. In miniature, it is easier to finish the yardarm by making a long (non-tapering) spigot at the end, so that a square block can be made to slide up the spigot, and then glued to the yard; the result of this is that there is a solid squared block which can be aligned, carved and machined. The shoulder section is milled or chiselled through from both sides, with the advantage that squared shoulders can be clamped accurately and easily into vice jaws. The shoulder sheaves appear on all the crossed yards, and the miniature iron banding is made from old-fashioned parcel tape, of the non-plastic variety.

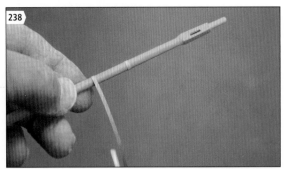

238

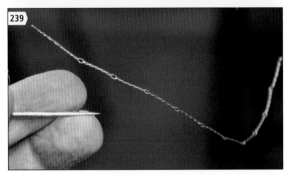

Banding the yards with 'iron hoops'. Just three turns of water-based parcel tape (not the shiny stuff) will give the effect required. Note that the shoulder sheave is fared off in line with the diminish of the yard. The advantage of using brown paper tape cut into fine strips is that although it is literally 'licked into shape', when the tape strip dries out, it also shrinks and grips bare wood with great tenacity. In case of doubt it also responds well to superglue, which soaks into it, and makes it extremely hard to remove. Just a couple of turns is all that is required to get the effect of iron banding, and because mid nineteenth-century practice used this reinforcement so often, it is an important technique to include.

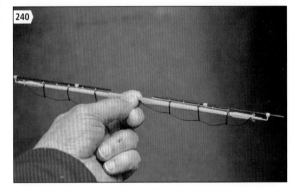

240

Top yard with fittings. Fittings to the yard include jackstay eyebolts, horses, stirrups and stunsail boom irons. In full scale, stunsails allowed for extra canvas to be spread in fair weather, with sails laced onto them. Fitting the eyebolts which secure the jackstay just calls for care and patience rather than huge amounts of skill. The iron/paper banding is a help, because the positions on top centre are easy to mark and an indent made to get the 0.07mm drill started. The banding also gives superglue a very good hold on the brass rings. Stirrups and horses made with copper wire are suspended from the jackstay irons. The wooden booms are referred to as stunsail booms (studding sails) and they slide into the boom irons. This makes provision for extra canvas in light airs.

239

Horses, stirrups, jackstays and stunsail fittings. In full scale, stirrups are short lengths of rope supporting the 'horses' (slack foot rope) on which crewmen have to stand for adjusting the sails. In miniature, copper wire is loosely spun up in the chuck of a hand-held brace, with just two strands, making it possible to force through a stirrup shape with a metal scriber. In the horses and stirrups which enable members of the ship's crew to move along the full length of the yard and work the canvas, the foot rope is left intentionally slack, so that it can always move through the loop of stirrups, and in full scale, up to half a dozen men would be using the foot rope to work the canvas; this was always a precarious manoeuvre, particularly at night. In the latter days of the merchant service, an extra grab-rail was fitted behind the jackstay called a safety stay, but these are not found on RN ships. The reason the foot rope is left slack is that sailors went barefoot, and a slack rope gives a better and kinder grip to the sole of a foot than a taut one. The stirrups are made by piercing them through to create an eye, soldering the strands either side of the eye and then trimming off; they are then fitted to the ring eyes on the yard with fine pliers so that the stirrup hangs freely on the aft side of the yard. Best to paint them before you fit them.

10: Iron Wire Rigging and the Ropewalk

241

242

241

Setting up the topgallant backstay to the fore channel. The wooden box is to tension the wire onto the backstay iron. The standing rigging for HMS *Gannet* used spun iron wire, a connection with both SS *Great Britain* and HMS *Warrior*. All three vessels enjoyed the advantages which this new material gave when compared with natural fibre rope, in terms of its strength and longevity. Its first real nautical introduction was aboard *Great Britain* in 1843, whose original aft masting system was designed by Brunel to be lowered onto the deck using hinged mast housings, streamlining the ship when under steam alone. It was an engineer's solution and bitterly resented by crew members, who complained of the wire's rigidity when compared with the pliability of natural fibres; nor could you handle it, splice it or make knots with it. Aboard *Great Britain* the wire was replaced in 1846 when the rig was heightened, this time using natural fibres throughout. The Admiralty, on the other hand, found that iron-wire-rigged ships required less maintenance, and wire therefore grew in popularity with them for this reason. It meant that only running rigging, which required the tight turns of sheaves and blocks, had to be replaced when routine checks were made, and providing the wire strands were well painted, greased or tarred, there was really no contesting the superiority of metal rigging. In short, wire rope was lighter, more durable and cheaper.

242

Miniature ropewalk component parts. *Tailstock end, left to right.* The sliding tailstock on aluminium bars, 12V (low) geared DC electric motor with forward and reverse plus speed control, via 12V transformer, (out of picture) a fixed driving hook gripped in a small chuck attached to the motor, fisherman's spinner plus loose hook on its fore end, to which all the strands are tied, wooden top with four grooves, four times two metallic thread strands tied up to the gearbox. Note that the three-grooved wooden top lies on the table. *Headstock end, left to right.* Homemade gearbox with 'sun and planet' wheels. On the axle ends of the cogwheels are attached five hooks. The outer ones will take three- or four-stranded rope as required, or any multiples of this combination. The centre cog is used for serving rope (see below). Between the drill and the gearbox, a universal coupling is fitted to lessen any vibration. Attached to the universal coupling is a mains-powered electric drill fitted with variable speed on its trigger, plus forward and reverse. The speed is controlled by a simple wood clamp. A foot switch is also fitted to the drill, used as a cutout when the rope is fully wound, and also in emergencies. The first stage of the procedure for manufacturing miniature rope is spinning the strands together; these will have been spun by the manufacturer either right- or left-handed, and loaded onto a bobbin or reel; it is important to establish the lay of the original manufactured strand. It can be untwisted at the end to find this out; if the strands point to the left, that is how it has been laid in the factory (left-handed), and vice versa. The direction of spin is given to the motor either forward or reverse, against the manufactured lay. This is the reason why both motors need forward and reverse.

243

Second stage: spinning the strands into rope. The strands are first attached by knotting them individually onto the hooks of the gearbox headstock at the right-hand end of the machine. The strands on the left-hand end at the tailstock are then tensioned and tied together into a single knot on the loose hook, attached to the front right-hand end of the fisherman's spinner. The tailstock unit is then pushed towards the left-hand end to provide tension for the whole length of the miniature ropewalk. At this point the wooden top is set at the tailstock end and the strands placed into its

242

grooves – either three or four strands, or any combination of this number. When all the strands are set in motion at the headstock end, the motor, turning against the manufacturer's lay, will at first spin all the strands together, until sufficient internal tension has been built up. At this point, the strands will start to turn in on themselves and rope will begin to form of its own accord, squeezing the nose of the top along the length of the rope. The top acts as a control on the apex where the strands come together forming the rope, and the pressure exerted at this culmination point will start to squeeze the top along the length of the rope as it is being formed. It does this of its own accord, moving by degrees towards the headstock. It works as though by magic! The top can be fixed to an overhead cable, which is the reason for the brass wheel attached to the opposite end, but I prefer to guide it by hand. When the rope is made, and needs to be hardened for the third stage of rope-making, the spinner is then hooked into direct drive, from the tailstock end. This can most easily be done by hooking up the eye on the front end of the spinner, attaching it directly onto the driving hook. This saves losing any tension or time, and is another reason for having a tail slide, provided by the aluminium slide bars. The third stage is called rope hardening. The

spinner is now used as a direct link at this point, hooking up to the motor. Power at low revs is then applied at the tailstock end to tighten all the strands of the rope together until it is hardened; this third stage forces extra tension on the newly made rope, binding it all tightly together. Finally, the spinner is hooked once more to the tailstock motor, and the tensioned rope will then unwind by itself, but only to the point where the miniature rope self-stabilises. One of the outcomes of the hardening process is to impart a certain amount of elasticity to the made rope. This liveliness is most helpful in that it tends to tighten rigging slightly of its own accord in a helpful way – a sign of the energy imparted into the manufacturing process.

244

Wooden top. The travelling top at the stage where the rope is being formed. Tension alone is pushing the top along the ropewalk. As the rope tension increases, it will slowly draw the tailstock carriage towards the headstock at the same time. This is a result of the rope shortening as it is made from the individual strands

243

244

245

Headstock and gearbox. The wooden top has been squeezed along to the limit of travel by the spinning process. As this forming of the rope is taking place, the carriage at the tailstock end will start moving down the slide, again of its own accord, because the rope will be shortening in length as it is being made. This is why the tailstock motor has to be mounted on a slide. Depending on the thickness of the material being used, this shortening of the rope can be as much as 20 per cent for thick material, or as little as 5 per cent for very fine strands. Without this sliding motion, the rope will simply fracture, and sometimes it does anyway, which can be an exercise in patience to repair.

246

Serving. The made rope is now being turned between the headstock and tailstock, with a long 'V'-groove placed under the rope. This attachment is set up beneath the wire rope at a gentle angle, and automatically (on a good day) wraps thread around the central core. Regarding worming and parcelling (in miniature, wrapping rope with thread), standing rigging on sailing ships always shows this outer wrapping of a natural fibre rope; in full scale, it is first 'wormed' with small-diameter cord pressed into the strands along the length of the rope to take out the high spots; it is then bandaged, or parcelled, to make a smooth surface, and finally wrapped with fine strand and coated with tar. This wrapping process can be achieved in miniature on the ropewalk by the addition of a 'V'-groove section, placed immediately below the length of rope being treated. A reel of wrapping cord will feed itself automatically onto a revolving length of rope, if it is weighted down onto the 'V'-groove with a metal bar through the centre of the cotton reel. The rope is driven by attaching the fisherman's spinner to the headstock gearbox; the driven end is powered from the tailstock at slow revs. Using the same principle, thread can be wrapped around a length of copper wire, which is very useful for covering strops and so forth in a realistic manner. The wrapped wire is then given a coat of shellac to stabilise the finish; this is most

easily done by using a short length of aluminium angle, taking a brush dipped in shellac along the back-side of the rope. By backing the rope in this way, it ensures the mixture can be applied back and front simultaneously. The distance between the headstock and the tailstock on the model ropewalk is immaterial; I normally set it at approximately 3m, but it can be much greater than this if required. It does not appear to alter the quality of the lay, which self-adjusts in terms of overall tension. The Ropery at Chatham Dockyard is approximately one-third of a mile long, and bicycles are still used to reach from one end to the other. The most I have ever tried on the model version is 50ft, outside the workshop. Using metallised thread is a new venture as far as my machine is concerned, and the result is interesting. It is perfectly possible to spin soft metal wire – light gauge copper wire or softened brass wire – of which you see examples used on the contemporary ship models of the mid-nineteenth century, but the downside is that if the spun wire is in anyway damaged in its later life, it kinks, and it is very difficult to straighten it out when it has been damaged. It is also far too strong for its own good, aided by the spinning process which automatically hardens it at the same time. To the rescue has come a product called metallic thread, which is basically a nylon thread with a filament of what I suspect is aluminium somehow processed into it. Metallic thread is available from haberdashery stores: my particular one is Coats silver metallic thread (301); it is right-hand laid in the factory, so has to be spun left-handed on the ropewalk. In terms of miniature realism, when it is spun up in differing diameters, it would be hard to beat; it looks exactly as it should and it has a secret bonus. It can be crimped together to give that realistic look of wire ends with proprietary crimping balls, as used by those crafting necklaces and beadwork. This simplifies the rigging process. It also provides the lighter look of iron-wire rigging which, in full scale, replaced much thicker rope. Compare the shroud rigging on HMS *Victory* (1765) with that of wire-rigged vessels of the nineteenth century, and the advantages become obvious. Not only is it stronger, but it gives much less resistance to a sidewind.

247

The swifter, technically the leading or forward shroud, is set up with the 'iron wire'. Setting up the rigging begins with fitting all the lower masts with shrouds; on the model, these have been individually tensioned to the internal chainwale plates (channels) and crimped into place. On the prototype, they have individual treble sheave blocks in place of deadeyes to tension the rigging, of a sort which are detailed on the ship's plan and were specially made by Nielsen's restoration team. The topmast rigging uses conventional deadeyes, tensioned down with lanyards in the traditional style.

248

Deadeye (rigged). Detail of the 'iron wire' wrapped around a deadeye and secured with crimps. When all the backstays have been secured to their fixing points, the forestays can then be spun up, served with thread and rigged; the order of placement has to follow a strict sequence, starting with the leading shroud and working aft; the forestays are then attached over the mastheads, looping over the shrouds in the style of a lasso and secured to the appropriate blocks.

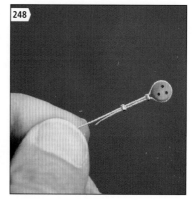

249

The complete (pre-rigged) mast being stepped with a crane, a Nielsen photograph from 4 June 2003.

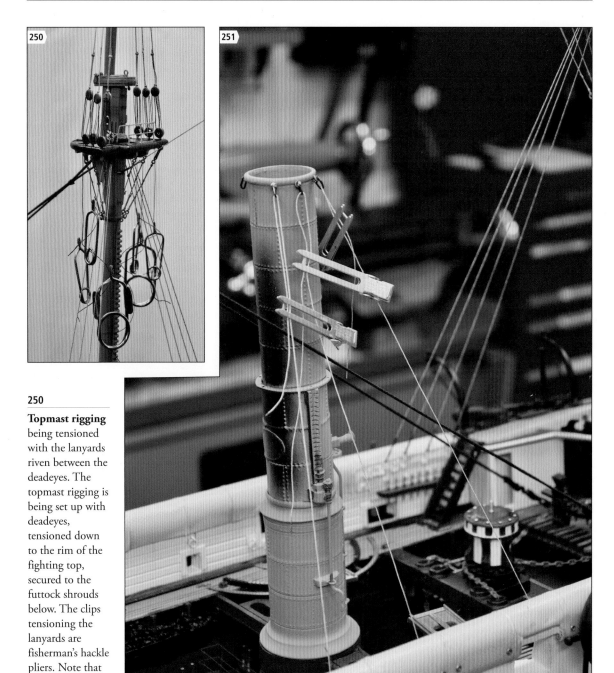

250

Topmast rigging being tensioned with the lanyards riven between the deadeyes. The topmast rigging is being set up with deadeyes, tensioned down to the rim of the fighting top, secured to the futtock shrouds below. The clips tensioning the lanyards are fisherman's hackle pliers. Note that the served rope of the forestay is rigged over the top of the shrouds; the normally hidden diagonal sheave for hoisting the mast heel out of its housing is clearly visible.

251

Funnel stays. These are made from very fine three-strand wire belayed to shackles on the funnel rim and secured to ring bolts on the bulwarks. Six of these are secured to the ring bolts in the ship's inner side and taken to the top rim of the funnel, secured with shackles and crimps. I suspect that the originals were made of chain, which would have made for easier handling when the funnel was raised and lowered, but I have made them as inconspicuous as possible, not wanting them to detract from the detail of the boiler room. It is a fact of life that rigging, both in miniature and in full scale, takes over visually from everything else.

252

Foremast topgallant shrouds. These
are rigged to the topmast collar;
although I am right-handed, that is
being used to grab hold of the ceiling!

253

Leathering the truss of the main yard.
Note the arrangement of the push-pin.
The upper yards are displayed in their
lowered position, as is correct for
harbour rig. The collar fittings to the
upper yards hold the central bunt of
the yard to the mast – yet another
reason why the bunt is given a flat
surface on its eighth-squaring – to
which the truss is attached. On the
model, the aft yoke, or keep, is made
by centring two ring bolts in place, into
pilot holes, with an indented copper
bar which acts as the keep; this is then
soft-soldered in situ for good
alignment. The advantage of having
this as a pin fitting is that the keep bar
can be pushed in and out when the
yards need to be released, which in the
initial stages of setting up the rigging is
quite often. The leathering is also
useful in that it neatly holds the yard
wherever it is placed on the upright
mast, simply by friction. In full scale,
Lieutenant Green's patent truss, which
was almost universally adopted after
1830, had a hinged fitting and a hasp,
keyed into place, but that would be
very fiddly to make and operate
compared with a two-pin push-fit.

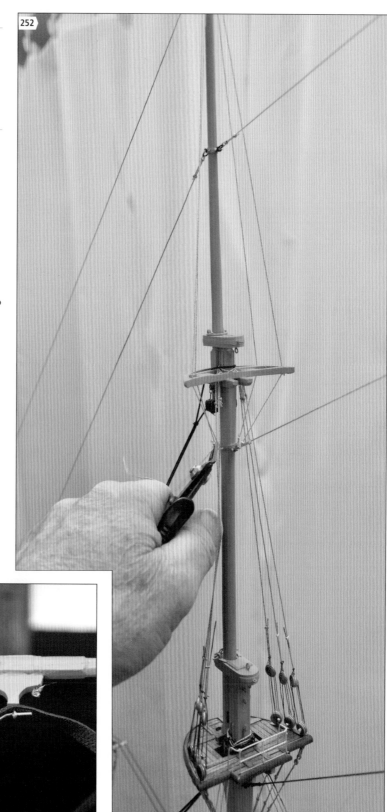

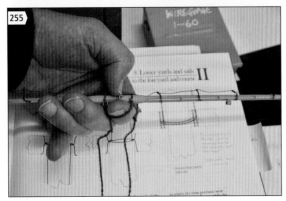

255

Chain truss pendant for the lower yard. The chain slings were wrapped twice around the central bunt and then suspended from blocks located under the lower trestle-trees, thence attaching directly to the bits on the deck below. The chains held these massive poles against the lower masts and were rigged in such a way as to allow for a limited arc of swing for the yards, and were self-adjusting by virtue of their own weight. There was no wooden collar involved.

254

Purchases and lifts. The lower lift purchases (rigging blocks with sheaves) give the ability to adjust both the height and the level of the yard; this particular style of purchase is known as an 'up and down', with a double block above a single block; the rope starts by being secured to the deck and is riven with a lengthy lanyard between the two blocks. To be correct, the distance between the blocks must be sufficient for the yard to be hauled to the correct height on the mast, so the lanyard is unusually lengthy when the yard is in its lowered position. The gearing ratio of the rigging blocks gives the lift a three to four times advantage in terms of the haul. The fore and main yards are not often moved from their raised position, being heavy and cumbersome; they are supported on a semi-permanent basis by the lifts, normally rigged into position when the ship was in the dockyard. By this date, merchant shipping of a similar size to *Gannet* would have iron-forged trusses secured to the lower masts, but those of the Royal Naval continued, even at this late stage, to be made from chain, known as pendants.

256

Chain sling and forged iron hook. Note the served double forestay leading down from the mainmast head. The iron hook attaches to the chain from the masthead cap: in full scale, it is normally 'moused' with a short length of rope to prevent the hook and eye parting. The chains are led to the underside of the fighting top, and then down to the deck bitts. There is a separate chain fitting which derives its support from being suspended from the mast cap, leading down on either side of the masthead in the style of a necklace to a wishbone fitting, then fed through the fighting top, and joined to a forged hook and eye at the central balance point of the yard. These three fixing points are what took the strains of the yard's deadweight and the forward pull of the sails. This virtually completes the standing rigging as far as I am taking it, apart from the addition of the ratlines and the sheer poles, whose job it is to keep the lowest rigged point of the shrouds in position. The ratlines in my case are made from fine spun copper wire, which allows for imparting the characteristic sag; knots are unavoidably over-scaled and cumbersome on ratlines, so a tiny spot of glue completes the job before they are blacked over.

257

The fully rigged yard in close-up (model).

258

Dockside view of the rigging on the model, before blackening the wire.

259

Ratlines. The ratlines are added to the shrouds and the standing rigging blackened. Note the effect of the differing thicknesses and gauges of wire.

260

Helm and poop deck completed. The 90cwt guns moved to the aftmost gun ports on their RCD carriages.

261

Fore quarter of the starboard side, 5 May 2017. The model ship is now mounted on keel blocks.

262

Internal detail completed. The guard-rails are added to the fo'c'sle and poop decks; note the chequered flooring of the wardroom.

263

The Union Flag flown from the jackstaff – handmade, with copper wire inserted into the top and leading edge.

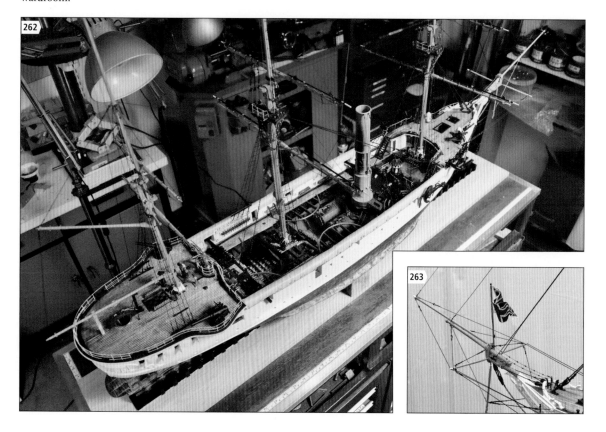

11: The Finished Model

Model ships need the protection of a case; no one really likes casing a model because it is like putting a bird in a cage, but there is no other option for keeping them safe and away from harmful dust. For a large model like *Gannet*, a professionally constructed case would be a very expensive item, and if it is glazed to the standards of health and safety now demanded by public display, it will more than likely involve a plate-glass construction supported by steel framing at its base. The alternative is a handmade timber frame using acrylic sheet. This is lighter in weight, but will scratch more easily and suffers somewhat from static dust. They are most effectively cleaned with a soft vacuum brush or chamois leather. If you are planning to make your own cabinet, you will need a circular saw to accurately cut the channels for the acrylic sheets to slide in, and without going into all the details of construction, because these will vary considerably, do start by making a mock-up of the corner jointing systems, marking up the detail and always being aware that the acrylic sheets need recessing and the corner joints reinforcing.

The corners are best made with a housing joint of some kind, glued with a triangular corner piece on three sides of the case, but not the front. The case is a large object, which is going to depend on the rigidity of the ply sheets at the top, bottom and back. The best design of case for a large model also includes being able to remove the front glazing bar, so that any model ship on a stand can be made to slide in and out of the case without endangering the masts. It is also a good idea to have the front panel(s) removable for viewing or photographing the model, so that provision for the easy removal of the panels needs to be carefully considered. A deeper channel slot on the top glazing bar will allow for this; the base needs only a shallow groove.

Internal lighting will be yet another issue. LEDs are now commonplace, and it is also possible to fit a dimmer switch to these. Added to all of this is the consideration of a background scene or colour which requires a plain backing board; this is superior for seeing the detail of rigging, etc, but if you decide on total 'glazing', be careful about reflection; it will work well enough when the illumination is coming from inside the case, but may give distortion looking through two layers of glass when the display case is unlit. You can also get back reflection from other light sources which create unwanted effects. Unless the model is to be displayed as a central feature of a room, it is better to use a plain backboard, which for lightness and strength should be made from plywood.

The framework of the display case is made from utile, technically a hardwood of the mahogany family, but fairly light and straight-grained. The timber has been treated with a graining effect of white liming wax and polished – easy to apply with a rag or brush, it takes out the yellow hue of this timber and is currently a fashionable finish, rather than darkly stained wood. The waxing agent is from Liberon UK – liming wax finished with clear Black Bison polish.

265

Case under construction.

264

Mock up of the corner joint showing the deep-cut groove for the top rail; the bottom rail should be as shallow as possible.

266

The author with the painted background of the display case. Seascape background is by Ben Mowll RSMA.

267

Gannet finally housed in the display case, lit with dimmable LED lighting.

268

Job done aboard HMS *Gannet*. They appear to have enjoyed their work as much as I have done mine. (Nielsen archive)

269

'Launch' photograph beside the waters of the Thames Estuary.

270

CGI image of the model. (Josh Mowll)

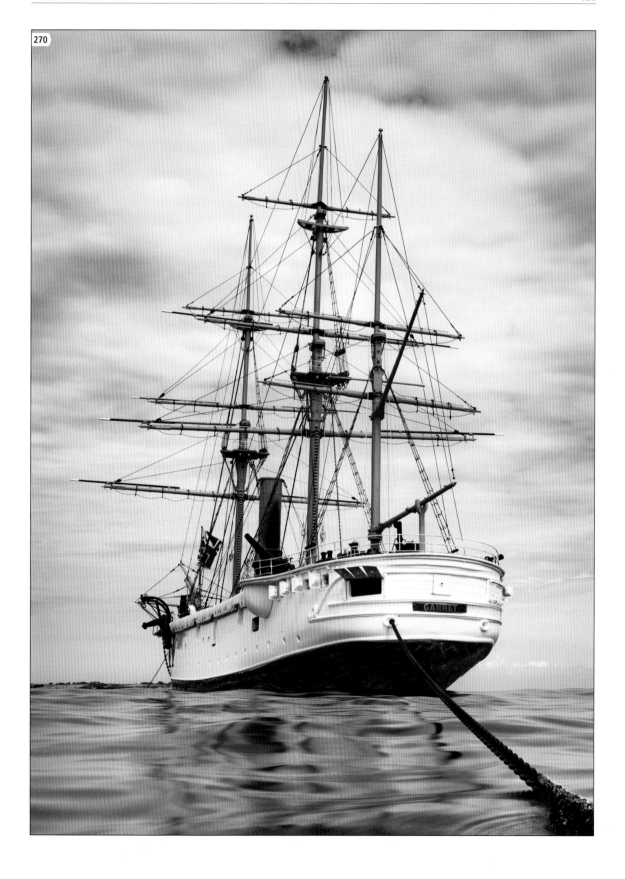

Conclusion

This often asked question of 'How long did it all take?' can now be answered. The simple reply is four years of retirement time, approximately three days a week. Building the vessel without writing down a record of what has taken place would no doubt shorten the process, but being aware that the camera will pick up on the slightest detail which may be badly made or historically incorrect is really what slows the process down. The internet is also a harsh taskmaster. I have no illusions about model ships; they are not to be compared with the originals which require the sweat of the brow, endless calculations and real courage to construct or restore, but model ships do have a dignity in their own right, as beautiful objects of both scientific and artistic interest, and most importantly, they contain the sweet dreams of those who are lucky enough to build them. That is their true worth.

How much money the model is worth is a much more difficult question to answer; if you calculate the time taken in research, the gathering of materials, correspondence, workshop costs, tools, insurance and experiment, it represents a frightening total, which I will leave you to calculate. On the open market you would not see a return of anything like your outlay. It all depends on who might want it, and what purpose it would be serving, but in general terms, making model ships will not make you rich in anything other than satisfaction. There are just a handful of professional model shipwrights left in this country, earning their living with their bare hands but never being able to hang on to their creations. As a hobby, model shipwrighting still thrives worldwide with the skills of many amateurs, and although I have worked on commission, and also sold and repaired various models, I am certainly still a perpetual student, hopefully learning each day one more thing than I forget.

The quartet of preserved transitional ships, *Great Britain*, *Warrior*, *Gannet* and *Discovery*, has had a great deal of money spent on them, and will be forever needing more. Old ships, like ancient buildings, are in constant need of repair and refurbishment, and do not do well by being anchored to one spot; as with all machines and machinery, despite wear and tear, they are much better in use than standing idle, but for these four exhibited vessels, their working life is now over, and not a single one of them will ever put to sea again, although they may appear ready to do so. This means two things – once they have truly astonished us with their magnificence, grace and charm, which they certainly do, they now mainly exist to educate us and inform future generations, reminding us all of the importance of our history, both in triumph and disaster.

It is difficult to imagine human history without the inclusion of water transport. Much of our language and phraseology is linked to sailing ships, because they have played so great a part in our ability to communicate vital information with speed and accuracy. Sailors spend much of their time in silence and contemplation, but when the wind shifts suddenly, or the link of a chain snaps, specific language is vital to saving the day and the situation. The mixture of history, art and science with these four surviving vessels make them, as a total collection, a unique reminder of our recent maritime past. To ignore them or destroy them is now unthinkable, because they are the key to understanding who our forebears were, what they achieved and who, as a result of those achievements, we have now become.

I have been privileged to build large-scale models of them all, and during their construction have gleaned so much information that has been worthwhile. I have also met some of their saviours and many of their present keepers, which is an experience that has enormously enriched my life, and I hope this translates into giving pleasure to many others.

William Mowll
August 2017

Glossary of Nautical and Mechanical Terms

Abaft
Sited behind.

Annealed
Metal softened by the application of heat.

Bandsaw
Powered, revolving, narrow endless saw blade, capable of cutting tight external curves.

Banjo frame
Apparatus by which the propeller of an auxiliary screw steamer is lifted and lowered in the screw well.

Beakhead
Area of the ship's head forward of the fo'c'sle.

Belaying pins
Removable pegs to which the running rigging is attached (belayed).

Bilge strake
Planking to which the bilge keel attaches.

Billboard
Horizontal baulk of timber in which an anchor fluke rests mounted on the foredeck ledge.

Bobstay chain
Acts as a back-guy to the upward pull of a bowsprit.

Boom
Any slender spar used for extending the foot of a (usually) triangular sail.

Bow chocks/anchor chocks
Baulks of timber fitted to the leading edge of the fo'c'sle deck.

Bowsprit
Large spar projecting over the stem of a ship; beyond is fixed the jibboom and the flying jibboom.

Brailed
Sail which has been hauled up close to the yard.

Breech-loader
Heavy gun which has a removable chamber on the aft end of the barrel, from which it is loaded.

Bulkhead frames
Main transverse divisions of a ship's hull; watertight bulkheads act as safety features and strengtheners.

Bull wheel
Final drive cogwheel gear in a lathe's headstock.

Bunt
Central portion of a yard, usually eighth-squared for extra grip and sometimes reinforced with battening.

Buttocks
Rounded or convex portion of the lower stern forming the transition from the stern to the flat side of a vessel.

Camber
Convex shape, usually applying to the surface of the deck or deck beams.

Cap
As applied to masting: strong block of wood with one square and one round hole, confining an upper and lower mast.

Capillary action
Where glue or solder is attracted by soaking into the stock or material being joined.

Capstan
Wood or metal barrel on a central pivot, worked with capstan bars and used for heaving or hauling rope or chain.

Cascabel
Round knob sometimes with an eye, on the aft end of a muzzle-loading gun – also known as a pommelion.

Casemate/embrasure
Chamber built to resist vertical fire, but through which heavy weapons may be deployed.

Cathead
Short projecting beam for lifting and lowering the anchor (catting).

Caulking
Forcing oakum and unravelled rope between planking with mallets, sealed with hot pitch.

Chain sling
Necklace of chain attaching and supporting the lower yards of a ship to the mast.

Channel (literally, chainwale)
Projecting longitudinal timber fixed to the ship's side walls, either inboard or outboard, as a fixing rail for the shrouds.

Cheeks
Also referred to as hounds: knee-shaped timbers in support of a mast-heel, fixed beneath the trestle-trees.

Cheese coupling
Means of detaching or engaging a lifting propeller with a male and female wedge-shaped coupling.

Cleat slots
Shaped sections of hardwood through which cabling may pass or be secured.

CNC
Computer numerically controlled.

Composite ship
Wooden ship built over iron frames.

Counter
Inwardly curved portion of the extreme after end of a vessel.

Cutwater
The upper end of the stem of a ship.

Deadeyes
Round blocks with three holes for adjusting the tension of standing rigging, riven through with lanyards.

Deep floors
Flooring in the fore and aft end of a vessel where the hull narrows.

Detente pin
Removable metal pin used for checking the motion of a dividing plate or other mechanism.

Dividing head
Lathe accessory for making divisions of a circle; can be used horizontally or vertically.

Dolphin striker
Short perpendicular gaff spar mounted beneath the bowsprit cap, attached to the martingale chain.

Doublings
Occur when the heel of the mast above is joined with the head of the one below, seated in the trestles.

Dowels
Round wooden fixings of various lengths and diameters.

Eighth-squaring
Octagonal section of a mast or yard giving extra grip and preventing twist.

Elliptical or round stern
The extreme after end of a vessel above the counter and abaft the stern-post.

Embrasure
See Casemate above.

Fighting top
Large demountable platform at the head of a lower mast used for many purposes.

Flask
A framed foundry box, originally using green sand for hot-metal mould-making from wooden patterns.

Flying jibboom
Outermost spar of the bowsprit.

Gaff
A spar, usually fitted with a jaw on the front (bottom) end, and to which a head rope may be attached.

Hackle pliers
Small clips used by fly fishermen who wish to make 'flies' from the neck feathers (hackles) of birds.

Hair bracket
See Head-rails.

Hawse pipe
(Pronounced 'hose-pipe'.) Cast-iron pipe to prevent cabling from damage when moored or riding at anchor.

Head ledge
The outer edge of timber or iron on a ship; can also be referred to as the cant edge.

Head-rails
The three curved and carved timbers extending back from the figurehead to the cathead.

Heads
Aboard ship refer to water closets/lavatories, seats of ease and urine dales (urinals).

Heart blocks
Triangular deadeyes with one large hole only, secured with lanyards.

Indexer
Engineering attachment used in conjunction with the milling machine/dividing head.

Ingate
Entry point of a mould/flask, into which the liquefied metal is poured.

Jackstaff
Short staff raised at the bowsprit cap, from which the Union Jack is hoisted.

Jibboom
Middle spar of the spike bowsprit.

Jigsaw
Powered piercing blade with reciprocating action; used for internal cutting.

Joggled
Deck planking let into the margin plank where the plank end is 'sniped' not less than half the plank's width.

Keel
Longitudinal member laid down on the ship's centre line to which all the frames are joined; ship's backbone.

Kerf
The incision made by the width of a saw-blade.

Knight-head
Iron casting into which the heel of the bowsprit is housed.

Lanyard
Short section of rope made fast to any item to secure it – mainly shrouds, deadeyes, back guys, etc.

Lifts
Rope supporting the lift of a yard from the masthead to the yardarm, belayed directly to deck bitts/lugs.

Magazine
Ammunition store – normally sited in both the fore end and aft end of a warship, below the waterline.

Margin plank
Surrounds the deck, placed alongside the waterway, into which the deck planking is joggled.

Martingale
Lighter gauge chain attaching to the dolphin striker; acts as a backstay for the jibboom.

Masts

Lower: fore, main and mizzen; topmasts: fore, main and mizzen; topgallants: fore and main only.

Maun pliers

Cantilevered pliers whose jaws work in parallel; much used by jewellers.

Metacentric level

Refers to the ship's stability and safety in reference to the righting of the hull when heeled.

Milling machine

Engineering apparatus with a fixed motor and milling chuck suspended over a mobile machine table. Milling machines are used for precise engineering tasks: slots, grooves, channelling, metal slitting, boring, drilling, etc.

Mitre fence

Device using the slots machined into the table of a powered bandsaw or table saw, to cut varying angles.

Muzzle-loading

Any gun which is loaded from the mouth of the barrel rather than the breech.

Ordnance

General term for heavy weapons or guns, either offensive or defensive.

Pawl rim

Notched circular base rim of a capstan which, when the pawls are engaged, prevent any 'running back'.

Pin rails

Shelves providing a housing for removable belaying pins, to which running gear is attached.

Pintles (rudder)

A ship's rudder is hung using braces (straps) and pintles.

Plank bender (model)

Copper tube with a heated flame running through the centre; soaked planks are formed thus.

Plank sheer

Narrow strake of planking placed on the upper edge of the sheer-strake.

Plans (ship's)

Referred to as lines plan, body plan, elevation, G/A plan view(s) of decks, inboard profile, midship section.

Plummer blocks

Cast-iron blocks resting on pedestals, on which the tunnel shafting either rests or revolves.

Poop deck

In *Gannet*'s case, a covered-over quarterdeck, providing a wardroom and cabin space for the commander.

Pooping sea

Heavy seas breaking over the stern quarters – extremely dangerous if the ship is heavily laden.

Propeller aperture

Space surrounding the lifting propeller where, on a sailing ship, the stern would meet the rudder.

Propeller boss

Central hub of the propeller. The boss plate is the swollen portion of the shaft at the stern.

Propeller shaft

Sealed tube in which the propeller revolves.

Purfling tool

Knife in handle used for incising tight curves; used for channelling the inlay of edging and decorative veneers.

Purchase

Strength, hold or leverage, particularly in terms of heaving and hauling through the use of block and tackle.

Quarter galleries

Originally a balcony with decorative windows on the quarters of a large ship.

Racer arcs

A protective rail set onto a ship's deck forming a horizontal arc on which a gun carriage traverses.

Radial arm saw

Powered circular saw, which runs in overhead rails for ripsawing, crosscutting, grooving, etc.

Ramin timber

Indonesian origin – much used for picture framing; straight grain but prone to splitting. Nasty smell.

Rebate

(Pronounced 'rabbit'.) Grooved joint to accept planking, with particular reference to that abutting the keel.

Riding bitts

Upright metal fixings to which the chain cabling is belayed when a ship is riding at anchor.

Roller fairleads

Ships' fittings shaped for semi-captive roping to pass through with ease, aided by a sheave (wheel).

Rudder-post

Supports the weight of the rudder and is sited immediately aft the propeller.

Scarph joint

Lengthy connection of two pieces of timber by overlapping their shaped ends.

Scroll saw

Reciprocating saw using a removable piercing blade for both internal and external cuts in wood or metal.

Scupper

Round or oval aperture for draining surface water off a ship's deck.

Sheave slot

Open mortice joint containing a sheave (wheel) through which a rope or 'stay' may be riven.

Sheer

The curve formed by the line of the upper deck at the side of a ship.

Shoulder sheave

The squared end of a yardarm, which provides greater strength to the sheaves.

Solder

Silver-solder requires high temperature with special flux; soft-solder uses soldering iron or open flame.

Soleplate

Heavy casting at the extreme end of the keel. Vital support to the rudder-post.

Spanker

Aftmost sail of a ship or barque.

Spigot

Short length of metal bar or timber.

Spile

Literally a narrow strip of timber, used as an infill.

Spleen

Flexible strip of timber, used for drawing lengthy shallow curves.

Spokeshave

Two-handled draw-knife originally for dressing the spokes of wheels and other internal curvature.

Stanchion post

Upright post supporting three guard-rails, removable when at action stations, often riven with chain.

Staples

Flat hooped bronze reinforcements attached vertically to the soleplate.

Stealer

Inserted strake of planking which does not extend from end to end of the vessel.

Steeved up

Referring to the upward-facing angle of the bowsprit.

Stem

Upright timber at the fore end of the keel.

Stern

Aftmost portion of the ship's hull.

Stern-post

Upright timber at the aft end of the hull – not to be confused with the rudder-post.

Strap linisher

Powered sanding machine using a revolving abrasive strap; the most used machine in my workshop!

TCT

Tungsten carbide-tipped.

Top

See Fighting top above.

Top yard

Yard crossing a topmast.

Trailboard

Carved board on each side of the stem, reaching back from the figurehead.

Transom plates

Internal plating supporting the structure of the counter at the aft end of the hull.

Truck(s)

The wheels of a gun carriage. Also the cap of topmost masts –'from keel to truck', ie the extreme height.

Vent piece

Removable breech block in front of which is placed the cartridge and shell/shot.

Waterline, or Load Water Line (LWL)

The line and depth to which the hull of a ship is submerged.

Wenge

Dense, dark brown African hardwood, coarse in texture.

Whelps

Ribbed fitting to the barrel of a capstan, for extra traction on roping to prevent slippage.

Yard

Timber crossing a mast from which a square sail can be hung.

Bibliography and Further Reading

SS *GREAT BRITAIN* (1843)

Ball, Adrian, and Diana Wright, *SS Great Britain* (David and Charles, 1981)

Corlett, Ewan, *The Iron Ship* (Moonraker Press, 1975)

Goold-Adams, Richard, *The Return of the Great Britain* (Weidenfield & Nicholson, 1976)

Mowll, William, *SS Great Britain: The Model Ship* (Argus Books, 1982)

Rowland, K T, *The Great Britain* (David & Charles, 1971)

HMS *WARRIOR* (1860)

Ballard, Admiral G A, *The Black Battlefleet* (Nautical Publishing Co, 1980)

Davies, Wyn, and Geoff Dennison, *HMS Warrior – Iron-clad frigate* (Seaforth, 2011)

Mowll, William, *Building a working model warship – HMS Warrior* (Chatham Publishing 1997)

Wells, John, *The Immortal Warrior* (Kenneth Mason, 1987)

SS *DISCOVERY* (1901)

Bernacchi, L C, *The Saga of the Discovery* (Blackie & Son, 1938)

Bryan, Rorke, *Ordeal By Ice* (Seaforth, 2011)

Fleming, Ian, *Model Shipwright*, No 31 (March 1980)

Mowll, William, Series covering the miniature build of SS *Discovery* model, *Ships in Scale* (Seaways, USA: 2012–13)

Savours, Ann, *The Voyages of the Discovery* (Virgin Books, 1994)

Scott, R F, *The Voyage of the Discovery* (1905; Penguin reprint)

Skelton, Judy, *The Antarctic Journals of Reginald Skelton* (Reardon Publishing, 2012)

Smith, W E (Superintendent), 'On the design of the Antarctic Exploration Vessel Discovery' (Admiralty papers and plans), *Transactions of the Institute of Naval Architecture*, vol 47 (1905)

HMS *GANNET* (1875)

Admiralty Specifications 1874 for a Single Screw Composite Sloop, of the *Cormorant* Class (Instructions for the building of a ship of this class 1–221)

Bound, Mensun, *The Archaeology of Ships of War* (Anthony Nelson, 1995)

Campbell, G F, *China Tea Clippers* (London, 1974)

Chatham Historic Dockyard Trust, HMS *Gannet* Conservation Plan (Nov 2000)

Doulton, Lindsay, Appendix D 'HMS *Gannet* survival and restoration', in Antony Preston, *Send a Gunboat*

Hughes, David T, *Sheerness Dockyard and Naval Garrison* (History Press, 2012)

Morris, Ronald, *The Captain's Lady* (Chatto & Windus, 1985)

Nutting, Anthony, *Gordon: Martyr and Misfit* (Chaucer Press, 1966)

Preston, Antony, and John Major, *Send a Gunboat* (Conway Maritime, 2007)

Walker, Fred M, *Ships and Shipbuilders: pioneers of design and construction* (Seaforth, 2010)

White, A L, *The Training Ship Mercury: A History 1885–1968* (The TS *Mercury* Old Boys' Association, 2003)

NINETEENTH-CENTURY STEAM ENGINES AND BOILER PLANT

Bourne, J, *A Catechism of the Steam Engine* (Longmans, 1850)

Gardiner, R, *The Advent of Steam* (Conway Maritime, 1993)

Griffiths, Denis, *Steam at Sea* (Conway Maritime, 1997)

Hawkins' Mechanical Dictionary (Theo Audel & Co, 1909)

Kennedy, J, *History of Steam Navigation* (Charles Birchall, 1903)

Lyon, D, and R Winfield, *The Sail & Steam Navy List* (Chatham Publishing, 2004)

Main, Thomas J, *The Marine Steam Engine* (5th edn, 1865)

Sothern, J W M, *Manual of Marine Engineering Practice* (12th edn)

Tucker, Spencer C, *Handbook of 19th Century Naval Warfare* (Sutton Publishing, 2000)

NAVAL ORDNANCE

Garbett, Captain H, *Naval Gunnery* (S R Publishers, 1897; 1971 reprint)

Masters, Roy, *The Royal Arsenal Woolwich* (History Press, 2010)

Padfield, P, *Rule Britannia –The Victorian and Edwardian Navy* (Routledge & Paul, 1981)

Perlmutter, T, *War Machines at Sea* (Octopus Lynx Press, 1975)

RIGGING AND SEAMANSHIP

Admiralty, *Manual of Seamanship* (1938)

Brassey, T A, *Naval Annual* (Griffin & Co, 1892)

Klinkert, J, *Compass-wise* (Brown, Son & Ferguson, 1976)

Lees, James, *The Masting and Rigging of English Ships of War 1625–1860* (Conway Maritime, 1979)

Lever, Darcy, *Practical Seamanship* (Longmans; reprint Algrove, Canada)

Nares, George, *Practical Seamanship* (Griffin & Co, 1897; 7th edn)

Paasch, Captain H, *Illustrated Marine Encyclopaedia* (1890; reprint Argus Books, 1977)

Underhill, Harold, *Masting and Rigging* (Brown Son and Fergus, 1946)

Walker, Captain T P (ed), *Captain Alston's Seamanship* (Griffin & Co, 1902)

ENGINEERING

Chapman, W, *Workshop Technology* (Butler & Tanner, 1985)

Harris, K N, *Model boilers and boiler-making* (Argus, 1978)

Sandham, R, and F R Willmore, *Metalwork* (Edward Arnold, 1979)

Trinder, B, *Britain's Industrial Revolution* (Carnegie, 2013)

Wright, P, *Model Engineering* (Melita Press, 2010)

List of Suppliers

Alec Tiranti: silicone rubber, sculptor's supplies, low melt metals, chavant, etc; www.tiranti.co.uk

Axminster Tools & Machinery: agents for Proxxon & Dremel; Lie Nielsen tools, etc; 1in belt and disc sander AW130BD2 (linisher); www.axminster.co.uk

BECC lettering: www.becc.co.uk

Chatham Historic Dockyard: www.thedockyard.co.uk

Chronos Ltd: engineering tools for model engineering: lathe chucks etc; chronos.ltd.uk

Dockyard Model Co, Florissant, Colorado, USA: miniature chisels and gouges; www.manta.com

Doll's House Emporium: miniature lighting, etc; www.dollshouse.com

Dremel: miniature drills and tooling; www.dremeleurope.com

EKP Supplies: small nuts, bolts, etc; www.ekpsupplies.com

Euromodels: wide variety of modelling supplies for scratch building; www.euromodels.co.uk

Fred Aldous: pewter and copper sheet; www.fredaldous.co.uk

Hegner UK: scroll saw Multicut 2; www.hegner.co.uk

Hobbycraft: craft supplies of all kinds; www.hobbycraft.co.uk

Jotika: model ship fittings, small chain, etc; www.jotika-ltd.com

K&S metals: miniature brass tubing and channelling, etc; www.ksmetals.com

Letraset transfers: etching name-plates, etc; letraset.com

Liberon: verdigris, French polish and other finishes, liming wax, etc; www.liberon.co.uk

Maidstone Engineering: brass, steel, sheet stock, etc; www.maidstone-engineeering.co.uk

Maplin: suppliers of electronic components; ferric chloride etchant; fine tools; www.maplin.co.uk

Maun: pliers (jeweller's); www.maun-industries.co.uk

Model Dockyard, Redruth, Cornwall: www.model-dockyard.com

Myford: Super 7B lathe and accessories; www.myford.com

National Maritime Museum: plans; www.nmm.ac.uk

Ottewill: jewellers and silversmiths; gold plating; www.ottewill.co.uk

Pebeo: Setacolor fabric paint; www.pebeo.com

Permagrit tools: diamond-coated profiling files; www.permagrit.com

Picreator Enterprises: Renaissance Wax; www.picreator.co.uk

Proxxon: milling machine; www.proxxon-direct.com

Rotring: drawing-board; www.rotring.com

Scientific Wire Co: copper wire, etc; www.wires.co.uk

Shesto: propane gas torch fittings; Sievert Classic Torch System (silver solder supplies); www.shesto.co.uk

SLEC: specialist timber supplies; Brazilian mahogany, Douglas fir, etc; www.slec.com

Titebond: aliphatic wood glue; www.titebonduk.com

Trimits: crimp beads; www.sewandso.co.uk

Tracy Tools: engineer's tooling, slitting saws; taps, dies, etc; www.tracytools.com

Weller: soldering iron systems (soft solder); www.wellersoldering.com

X-Acto: X-acto blades are available at most art and craft shops, also at Axminster Power tools; razor saws (miniature); www.Xacto.com